NORTHEAST
PHILADELPHIA

NORTHEAST
PHILADELPHIA

A BRIEF HISTORY

DR. HARRY C. SILCOX &
FRANK W. HOLLINGSWORTH

THE
History
PRESS

Published by The History Press
Charleston, SC 29403
www.historypress.net

First published 2009
Second printing 2013

ISBN 978.1.5402.2054.7

Library of Congress Cataloging-in-Publication Data

Silcox, Harry C., 1933-
Northeast Philadelphia : a brief history / Harry C. Silcox and Frank W. Hollingsworth.
p. cm.
Includes bibliographical references.
ISBN 978-1-5402-2054-7
1. Northeast Philadelphia (Philadelphia, Pa.)--History. 2. Philadelphia (Pa.)--History.
I. Hollingsworth, Frank W. II. Title.
F158.68.N67S537 2009
974.8'11--dc22
2009045616

This book is dedicated to all the former Lincoln High students who were our friends and colleagues in days gone by. May this book evoke fond memories of the neighborhoods we all knew so well in our youth.

CONTENTS

CONTENTS

PREFACE

The columns in the *Northeast Times* entitled "Living in the Past" are the basis for this book. Editor John Scanlon's idea to explore the social history of Northeast Philadelphia on the second and fourth Thursdays of the month has been well received by the people of Northeast Philadelphia. Reporter Diane Prokop has been the most supportive and helpful person on staff. She is a true professional with an understanding heart. Extremely popular in the region, these articles have sparked a new interest in the history of Northeast Philadelphia of which John Scanlon must be proud. In concert with a group of northeast historians, these articles have done much to stimulate a renewed interest in how people lived in the past. Active members of this new northeast historical group include Louis M. Iatarola, Fred Moore, Maxwell Rowland, Bruce Conner, Rosemary Clayton, Harvey Cantor, Edwin S. Moore and Gerard St. John; they have all contributed in their own way to this book.

Most crucial to the work was my co-author Frank Walker Hollingsworth, who was instrumental in researching materials in the northeast. Frank's interest and knowledge of Torresdale added greatly to the large section found on Torresdale in the book. He has become an expert on the area. The book could not have been published without his help. The co-authorship indicates his commitment and energy to the project. He is primarily responsible for the research material at the end of the book. During my current illness, Frank has been both supportive and helpful. A special thank-you goes to Hannah Cassilly for her advice and counsel in helping to develop the basic chapter outline for the book.

Bob Hollingsworth added his editing skills to improve the final version of the manuscript, and Bruce Silcox placed the manuscript in its final content form. Bruce and his daughter, Veronica Hayes, remained my number one supporters and fellow historians during the process of putting the book together.

Dr. Harry C. Silcox, Co-Author
2009
Elected to the Inaugural Northeast Philadelphia Hall of Fame

CHAPTER 1

OUT OF THE WILDERNESS

***

How Northeast Philadelphia Got Its Name

When Thomas Holme, William Penn's surveyor, mapped out his design for Philadelphia, he drew a rectangular city between the Delaware River and the Schuylkill River and between what are now South Street and Vine Street. Streets were formed into square block patterns with five sections of land set aside for parks, making it into William Penn's image of Philadelphia as a "a green country town." Philadelphia eventually became a township located in the county of Philadelphia in the state of Pennsylvania. There was no Northeast Philadelphia at the time. The area where Northeast Philadelphia is located today was composed of Moreland, Dublin, Oxford, Byberry and Lower Dublin Townships. Early settlements begun by Quakers in Lower Dublin, Oxford and Byberry Townships organized themselves into small villages. Much of the remaining land was divided into farms no smaller than fifty acres. A town in these early days consisted of institutions that offered farmers the necessities of life: a small church, a general store, a blacksmith shop and a gristmill that made flour for the home or bakeries. Among these early villages were Five Points, Mechanicsville, Smithfield, Bustleton and Holmesburg. By far the largest populated region was centered in Frankford Borough, which soon became the focal point of the region.

During the Revolutionary War, this northern suburb of Philadelphia became the food basket for both the British and American armies. Washington used the area to feed his troops before the Battle of Trenton, and British troops occupied Frankford on many occasions just to get rations for their army. One of Frankford's original industries was the production of gunpowder needed for the muskets of the day. This was dangerous work since the smallest spark could ignite the gunpowder, causing injury or death to the worker. The Frankford industry was quite large for the time, rivaling the famous DuPont Gunpowder Mill in Delaware. The large number of skilled gunpowder workers in Frankford led the United States government to open an army gunpowder facility in 1816. Named the "Frankford Arsenal," the gunpowder mill was located on the Delaware River near Bridesburg. This eliminated the danger of explosions in Frankford's village setting and at the same time made use of the supply of skilled gunpowder workers in Frankford.

The region remained a farming area into the 1820s. It was about then that disease outbreaks in the city made owning land in the country more desirable. Wealthy Philadelphians soon began to purchase summer homes in the northeast so that their families could escape the summer heat and diseases that often plagued the city.

This all changed in 1854 when many city officials began seriously discussing the county boundary of Philadelphia becoming the city boundary. There had been several unsuccessful attempts at this kind of consolidation before 1854, but they had all failed. The main opposition to these plans came from the Whig Party. The Whigs usually dominated Philadelphia elections, while the outlying townships were dominated by the Democrats. The Whigs feared that they would lose power within the city if the local townships were included as part of the city vote. By 1854, the political issues surrounding consolidation were taking a back seat to the more pressing problem of violence.

The arguments for consolidation now rested on the various townships' inability to govern. Law enforcement practices in the townships made it difficult to keep the peace. A person could break the law in Philadelphia and quickly cross the border and escape punishment. Districts outside Philadelphia could not control their criminal elements and at the same time refused to let Philadelphia get involved. An example of how poorly law enforcement agencies worked together came in May 1844 when an anti-Catholic riot erupted in Kensington. The sheriff was the only police officer available in Kensington at the time, and when Philadelphia's militia was called it hesitated because it had not been reimbursed for past services. By the time the militia arrived, the riot was out of control, resulting in twenty dead and hundreds wounded, as well as an 1845 law requiring the townships around Philadelphia to maintain adequate law enforcement.

This law proved unsuccessful when a riot broke out in Moyamensing in 1848 and there were no law enforcement personnel available. A gang from another part of town had to be hired to stop the riot. A new 1850 law was then passed that gave Philadelphia authority over law enforcement in the seven districts that surrounded the city. This did little to solve the problem since Philadelphia had no police force at the time.

None of this bothered the farmers of what was then Northeast Philadelphia. Farmers liked the idea of being left alone with few taxes needed to provide services for water, waste removal and control of the criminal element. As far as crime was concerned, farmers took care of that issue by banding together to quell whatever outbreak occurred. As for water, they had their own wells, and for waste, their own outhouses. The Consolidation Act of 1854 was written to enable the city to work better, not the countryside.

With the support from the city's major newspapers, the Whig opposition to consolidation was overcome, and the matter was taken to the Pennsylvania state legislature for action. Eli Kirk Price brought the issue to the Pennsylvania Senate, while Matthias W. Baldwin did the same in the House of Representatives. The bill passed both houses on January 31, 1854, and was signed into law by Governor William Bigler. The Consolidation Act of 1854 also had a provision that gave greater executive power to the mayor, who was to be elected every two years. A permanent police force was ordered by the mayor using his new authority as provided in the law. On March 11, Philadelphia celebrated the Consolidation Act with an excursion on the Delaware River, a ball at the Chinese Museum and a banquet at the Sansom Street Hall, all with Governor Bigler in attendance.

In an editorial entitled "The New City," Philadelphia's *North American* expressed the sentiments of most elite Philadelphians, stating, "We can scarcely find words in which to adequately express that profound and earnest sense of gratification which we feel at the final triumph of Consolidation." Overnight the city had grown from 2 to 130 square miles with a population increase from 121,000 to 409,000. This also gave Philadelphia the distinction of having the largest area of any city in the United States.

While Philadelphia officials and residents celebrated receiving funding from the Consolidation Act of 1854, which allowed them to hire a police force, the farmers of the northeast townships found little to be happy about. The fear of increased control over their region by the city and increased tax burdens were reminders that they were less independent than before consolidation. A survey of citizens in Byberry Township in 1854 indicated a six to one majority against consolidation with the city. It was clear that Byberry at the time would rather have become part of Bensalem in Bucks County.

The leaders in favor of consolidation in Northeast Philadelphia were African American Robert Purvis and James P. Verree, both men who had friends and contacts in Philadelphia. Purvis had his life threatened in the city riots of 1842 before moving to Byberry to be near his brother, a Bensalem farmer. Purvis held the position that safety for the city was a necessity and that consolidation would also bring benefits to the people in the suburbs. Verree supported the need for a police force in the city because those same police could also be used to quell riots in suburban townships. During debates in Bustleton and Holmesburg in 1852, Samuel C. Willits challenged Verree, taking the side of the farmers of Byberry and Upper Dublin Townships who saw no benefits for them from the consolidation of the city and townships. Willits defended his position in 1884, stating that "thirty years have expired since the 1854 Consolidation Act was passed and so far as rural properties have been affected, it has not been favorable to them."

These feelings toward the city, though they seemed to disappear, never really went away. Peter Binzen, writing in Murray Friedman's book *Philadelphia Jewish Life 1940–2000*, describes the farmers of 1920 living near Oxford Circle as "wanting to be left alone without additional tax burdens." But cities required increased government control and more taxes as they grew in size. In the 1970s, Northeast Philadelphia politician State Senator Frank Salvatore called for Northeast Philadelphia to secede from Philadelphia and become Liberty County. This was viewed by many as an extreme resolution, but it did reflect the feelings of many Northeast Philadelphians who still remembered the historically condescending relationship of the city toward them.

The importance of the Consolidation Act of 1854 to Philadelphians today was that it brought to the city a new terminology for describing sections of the city. No longer was the use of the term "township" necessary to describe an area of the city. Far easier was the general use of descriptions like South Philadelphia, West Philadelphia, North Philadelphia and Northeast Philadelphia. From this point in time, Northeast Philadelphia officially existed and was a clearly identified, easily located part of Philadelphia. Still, where Northeast Philadelphia began and where its central population core was located remained a mystery.

Northeast Philadelphia in the 1860s was located in the heart of Kensington and remained there into the 1920s. When the first high school was built in Northeast Philadelphia, it was at Eighth and Lehigh Streets in the heart of where Kensington is today. Like the location, it was called Northeast High School.

Also, the borough of Frankford should not be confused with Northeast Philadelphia. Frankford was a commercial town that developed its own industries and became rich through these industries by selling goods and services to Northeast Philadelphia farmers. Nevertheless, Frankford leaders spent much of their time and effort in improving the connections to center city Philadelphia. One only has to study the improvements in transportation to center city to realize the time and energy extracted from the community to get this done.

Transportation to the city from Frankford began with an early stagecoach route and then progressed to a horse-drawn coach on rails, a Dummy steam car on rails, electric trolleys and, finally, the high-speed elevated lines. Each improvement in transportation decreased travel time to the city and cemented Frankford's claim as the commercial center of Northeast Philadelphia. This decreased travel time moved the population center of the northeast from Kensington to the area adjacent to Frankford.

In 1912, when a high school was needed for the increased population of the northeast, it was built in Frankford. By the 1920s, Frankford and its adjacent areas had become the center of what people then called Northeast Philadelphia. By the 1930s, the high-speed elevated line moved the center for Northeast Philadelphia farther north into the open fields at Cottman and Bustleton Avenues, and new residential construction in what is now Mayfair moved the center of Northeast Philadelphia population farther north. When a new high school was built in 1958, the name Northeast High School was removed from the building at Eighth and Lehigh Streets and placed on the new building at Cottman and Algon Streets. This was done based on the argument that Kensington was no longer in Northeast Philadelphia.

The building of I-95 in the 1970s and the opening of three exits into Northeast Philadelphia (Cottman Street exit to Mayfair, Academy Road exit to Torresdale and the Woodhaven exit to Byberry) now extended the center of population for Northeast Philadelphia to near Grant Avenue and Academy Road. Frankford was no longer considered part of Northeast Philadelphia, like Kensington; time had eroded its claim to being in Northeast Philadelphia. No longer was the northeast dependent on Frankford for services, leaving it an economically depressed area with a manufacturing base that soon dried up and died. So it is today that Northeast Philadelphia is generally described by politicians, street maps and residents as the area above Frankford that begins with Wissinoming. It is doubtful that the location of Northeast Philadelphia will change in the future because there is no land left that would allow the city to expand.

***

HOLMESBURG: THE ORIGINAL VILLAGE

It is clear from the beginning of Northeast Philadelphia that the building of churches and fostering of religion were primary goals for the formation of a new civilization. To civilize the wilderness, churches were deemed a necessity. Samuel Willits writes that there were members of three religions in early Northeast Philadelphia: Quakers, Episcopalians and Baptists. He added that "these three churches conveyed a better Idea of the state of the country, than could be obtained from any other source." One only has to look at the grandeur of the Emmanuel Episcopal Church and the Pennypack Baptist Church still standing today to understand that the Quakers were the least successful religious group in Holmesburg. As we discuss leaders of the town, many will prove to be Baptist, like founder John Holme, or Episcopalian, like Edward Duffield. To them, the wilderness could best be civilized through religion.

Holmesburg quickly became an area where wealthy landowners were bound together with low-paid laborers in the mills along the Pennypack Creek. How these groups worked together to promote a livable society is crucial to understanding early Holmesburg. By listing these institutions in chronological order, it is possible to view how this orderly society grew and prospered.

The first institution advocated by these early leaders in 1684 was a school. In that year, the will of Thomas Holme, Penn's surveyor, gave four pounds to Dublin Township to establish a school. Silas Crispin, Holme's son-in-law, was executor for the will, but he died without making a provision for this clause. In 1723, his son, Thomas, with the other heirs purchased two acres of ground for a school at what is today the intersection of Academy Road and Frankford Avenue. The first log cabin school of Holmesburg was built on this site in the 1790s. The trustees, led by Edward Duffield, and Principal Strickland Foster applied for a state charter, which was granted in 1794. The school quickly grew and prospered. In 1834, female pupils were admitted, making the school available to the entire community. A new building was constructed in 1808 and remained under the direction of the trustees of Lower Dublin until it was taken over by the public school directors in 1841.

The next phase in the development of the region was the building of the old gristmill on the Pennypack Creek near the King's Highway (Frankford Avenue). Built by the early Swedes prior to 1697, the water-powered grinding stones of the mill turned wheat into flour and corn into cornmeal, providing food for the area. For six decades, the mill brought rich and poor people together for their most essential item: bread.

During its most productive years in the early 1800s, the mill owned by George Pennock was the only available mill for the inhabitants of Bridgeport and other New Jersey towns. The Delaware River was filled with boats daily that were destined for the Pennypack Creek and the mill on Frankford Avenue. The mill was not only used by New Jersey men but also by the Welsh settlers above Bustleton, who came on horseback, forming a trail through the woods that eventually became Welsh Road. The Welsh usually came in armed groups with loaded rifles—their trips were dangerous because of predatory Native Americans and renegade white men. The mill remained in constant use, employing machinery in accordance with the times, until 1880, when a fire burned

Lower Dublin Academy was the first school in Holmesburg, built in 1808 utilizing stone from the Holmesburg Quarry. In its time this building was one of the finest schools in Philadelphia.

the woodwork and ruined the machinery. After the 1880s, the old race continued to empty its waters into the mill, forming a cascade over the broken machinery and wrecked millstones.

At about the same time, the local farmers began building a three-arched bridge over the Pennypack Creek on Frankford Avenue. Built between 1697 and 1698, it remains today America's oldest stone arch bridge still in use. Once completed, Frankford Avenue became part of the eastern roadway connection between New York and Philadelphia. The increased traffic on the highway led investors to build the first hotel in Holmesburg. In 1745, work was begun on a hotel that included ten rooms and an ample dining area to feed twenty-five guests. Located on Frankford Avenue a short distance from Pennypack Creek, the hotel had an area in which horses could be watered as travelers dined. It was named the Washington Hotel in 1790 in honor of George Washington, who had stayed there before and during the war.

Yet another institution established in Holmesburg was the Oxford and Lower Dublin Township Poor House, built in 1805 on the grounds now occupied by Lincoln High School at Ryan and Rowland Avenues. Despite Holmesburg having few factories at the time, the nearby residents of Frankford were in desperate need of a home for the families of workers who had been seriously injured or killed on the job. Frankford was the center of the gunpowder industry during the Revolutionary War and had a long history of explosions and accidents in its gunpowder mills. The gunpowder industry was moved from Frankford in 1814 when the United States government opened the Frankford Arsenal. The poorhouse in Holmesburg opened before there were any industries in Holmesburg but grew in importance to local residents as mills were built along the Pennypack Creek. The poorhouse was supported by a tax levied on all Oxford and Lower Dublin Township residents. The tax-supported home indicates the commitment that the local wealthy landholders had in providing help for the working class.

One of the major changes to Holmesburg occurred when two factories opened on Pennypack Creek. The Rowland brothers were the first to build a factory on the creek. They were experienced mill men, having produced the first saws made in America in 1805 in their Cheltenham, Pennsylvania mill. Jonathon Rowland decided to move his mill to the Pennypack Creek in 1829 to gain needed water power. A water raceway was built and a water wheel installed to provide

Oxford and Lower Dublin Township Poor House, built to accommodate the Frankford families of workers from their gunpowder industry who had been injured in accidents.

power for the factory. With the help of his son, Maxwell, Jonathon built a thriving business in Holmesburg. The Rowland mill on the Pennypack served the area farmers for the next century, producing steel farm tools. In the twentieth century, the factory produced shovels that were distributed throughout the world. Rowland Shovel Works was so proficient in shovel-making that it won first prize for the best shovel made for the 1876 Bicentennial Exhibit in Philadelphia. The workforce usually ranged from thirty to fifty employees, with most of the Rowland family being near the factory in houses built on the banks of the Pennypack Creek. The contributions of the Rowland family to Holmesburg can be found in Samuel C. Willits's manuscript. He claimed that the Rowlands were responsible for prosperity in Holmesburg because of their fair hiring practices and treatment of men during depressions.

A second factory opened on the Pennypack Creek in 1832 when Joseph Ripka, a Manayunk textile factory owner, opened a mill near where Rhawn Street is today. Seeking to diversify and enlarge his textile business, he sent his son Albert (age twenty-two) and nephew Andreas Hartel (age twenty-four) to Holmesburg to run the business. A dam was built a half mile upstream, and a raceway was constructed to power two wheels: one for the cotton mill and one for the printing mill. This was no small undertaking. The buildings were quite large for that era. Over one hundred workers from Holmesburg produced 750,000 yards of cotton goods. The cotton mill capital was reported

Holmesburg Calico Print Works in 1900 after it was closed. It was built in 1832 and managed for years by Andreas Hartel, whose house was on the creek where Hartel Street is today; the street bears his name.

to be $80,000. The print works had eighty workers and a capital of $160,000; the total worth of the mills combined was nearly $250,000. Houses were constructed for the workers on the west bank of the creek and near the original bridge built over the Pennypack to connect the mill residents to Holmesburg. In 1852, after the death of his eldest son, Ripka decided to quit his Holmesburg venture, selling the print works to Andreas and Albert Hartel. Andreas took possession of the entire factory in 1857 when Albert decided to return to Manayunk to work with his father. Hartel built his house next to the factory on the banks of the Pennypack, where he lived until the factory closed in the 1880s. Lorin Blodget, writing about Philadelphia industry in 1883, reported that "A. Hartel and company employed five printing machines which printed an average of 12,000,000 yards of calico cloth per year." Despite this report, Hartel Print Works would go out of business by the 1890s because of the many textile mills in Kensington.

Businessman Samuel C. Willits with partner George Courtney opened yet another factory on the Pennypack Creek in the 1840s. Born in Northern Liberties in 1819, Willits established a mill on the north bank of the Pennypack Creek adjoining the Rowland Shovel Factory. He built a flour and linseed oil mill and ran the business with his brother. He became interested in politics after a decade of working at the mill and was elected chairman of the local school board. In 1858, he became one of the early elected officials of the Republican Party as a common councilman from the twenty-third ward. He organized the Union Library and Literary Society in Holmesburg and joined the trustees of the Lower Dublin Academy. His historical writings remain today one of the best records of the time. He died in 1885, leaving his history unfinished. Clearly, from the earliest days, the wealthy class in Holmesburg recognized its responsibilities to foster education and civic improvements.

Despite being a center for manufacturing, the Pennypack Creek retained its idyllic splendor. Along its banks, John Audubon first studied and painted birds. World-famous ornithologist Alexander Wilson used the birds of the Pennypack in his categorical listing of birds. It was there, too, that James Greenleaf Whittier did his writing in the summers of 1838–39. The area retained its natural beauty in an unsullied form throughout these early years. For those who love nature, it remains today one of Philadelphia's most natural settings.

***

Bringing Learning to the Wilderness

The history of libraries in the United States tells much about the intellectual development of the nation. When settlers arrived in America in the seventeenth century, they carried few books besides the Bible. The primitiveness of the new frontier forced them to bring only essential items like household utilities, tools for cutting trees and seeds for growing food. Recognizing a need for discussions and books, no less a man than Benjamin Franklin organized a group of men into a "Junto." They met weekly to discuss the events of the day in Philadelphia during the 1730s. It was not long before they became frustrated by the few books available. To solve the problem, Benjamin Franklin proposed the first library in the colonies. His scheme was simple: Each member of the company would pay a monthly fee for books to be purchased in Europe and brought to Philadelphia to become part of a Library Company. Any book could then be borrowed for one week at a time by any contributing member. This lending library, available only to a wealthy few, set a pattern for early libraries in this country.

The first local community to imitate Franklin's library company was in Northeast Philadelphia. In 1794, a meeting was held at the Byberry School House for citizens who had previously met to organize the school. They resolved to "use their influence to promote a library in Byberry." It was decided to immediately open such a library in the home of Ezra Townsend of Bensalem. By December of that year, a constitution had been adopted and signed by twenty-nine citizens of the area. Among them were names still familiar to us today as street names in Byberry: Ezra Townsend, John Comly and Paul Knight. In 1798, the library was moved from the house of Ezra Townsend to the schoolhouse. In 1799, the rules were revised to allow the community greater access to the books. This system lasted until 1916, when books were removed to Joshua Gilbert's store during the rebuilding of the schoolhouse. The work was completed in 1918, and the books have remained there ever since. Although the library contained only three thousand volumes, the collection was carefully chosen to contain history, poetry, science, literature and art. Works by Prescott, Bancroft, Bryce, Lord Bacon, Kingsley, Emerson and Carlyle were all to be found in the library, quite a feat for this small, isolated farm community removed from city life. The library was so successful that local leader Nathan Middleton and his friends set up a fund, the interest from which provided money to purchase books each year, thus freeing the original stockholders from any annual payment.

Closely tied to the library was the Byberry Philosophical Society, which met and housed its collection in the same room. The society was formed in 1829 for "the acquisition and promotion of scientific knowledge," and its minutes show that it was at one time actively engaged in scientific investigations and acquiring Native American artifacts. Many of the birds and animals still in the collection were mounted by Charles Comly and Dr. Isaac Comly, both skilled taxidermists of that time. Isaac Comly later wrote a manuscript, *History of Byberry*, that formed the basis of Martindale's book on the area, *History of Byberry, and Moreland*. The large collection of waterfowl is still in the library and was a gift of Nathan Middleton. An additional case of animals and birds was the gift of Isaac Comly's wife, Elizabeth. Near the library was Thomas Shallcross's home, the Pines. His love of learning and positions as president of the Twenty-third Ward School and member of the Philadelphia School Board made him the prime supporter of educational opportunities in Byberry. A school bearing his name remains in the community to this very day.

Byberry Library, located in the Quaker Byberry School House. It remains today much like it is in this early picture.

A second library was formed in Northeast Philadelphia in 1823 when a group of civic-minded men met in Holmesburg. Benjamin F. Crispins, Jonathon Rowland and Dr. W. Scott Hendrie formed a lending library to be housed by Hendrie. Hendrie lived next to a Methodist Episcopal church near the center of town, and his informal library was well known to the better-educated families. Hendrie was an army surgeon and a colonel in a regiment of local Pennsylvania volunteers. He had a large practice and was extremely popular socially in Holmesburg. Through his efforts, a large number of books were collected that officially became the Holmesburg Library in 1867. To support the library, Dr. James Burd Peale (the Peale House at Welsh Road and Frankford Avenue is named after him) of the board of trustees of the Lower Dublin Academy obtained consent from the court that surplus income from the trust could be used to support the Holmesburg Library. Despite Peale's work, Hendrie was named the first president of the library. With full support from owner Benjamin Crispin, the books were moved to the newly opened "Athenaeum" building on Frankford Avenue the same year. An early report by Hendrie showed that the library contained two thousand books on shelves; six thousand books

Celebration in 1906 dedicating the Holmesburg Library at Hartel Street and Frankford Avenue.

were taken out annually. When Hendrie passed away in the late 1860s, Benjamin Crispin became library president; the librarian was J. Edger Morrison, who lived nearby. In 1880, the Holmesburg Library was formally accepted by the trustees of the Lower Dublin Academy, who provided continual financial support. The trustee minutes indicate that $300 was contributed yearly to buy new books.

The Athenaeum building remained the home of the library until 1906, when an Andrew Carnegie Grant built the current library at Hartel Street and Frankford Avenue. The trustees of the Lower Dublin Society purchased the land to meet Carnegie's requirement that land be given to obtain his grant. On the day the books were moved, over one hundred Holmesburg residents appeared at the Athenaeum to carry four thousand books four blocks to the newly erected library on Hartel Street. This festive and happy day of work ensured that books would continue to be available to the community.

Frankford was the largest community in Northeast Philadelphia at the time and also developed a library during the same period. The Friends Hospital built the first library in Frankford in 1832 for the exclusive use of patients. The Friends continued to add new additions to its hospital, making it an innovator throughout Northeast Philadelphia history. The earliest record of a "public" Frankford library appeared in an 1831 article when a group of citizens spoke of sharing their book collections. When Joseph Wright built the Wright Institute in 1854, he provided free space for a library room "with heat and light to be used perpetually as a reading room and library." Located at Griscom and Unity Streets, this library remained in the Frankford community until the Wright Institute closed in the twentieth century and a public library was built.

Another early library in Northeast Philadelphia was located in Tacony. The first thoughts of a public library for Tacony came in 1876, when a public meeting was held and the Keystone Scientific and Literary Association formed on October 24. Meetings were held weekly, at which debates, recitations and readings were given. The group met in the original schoolhouse at State Road and Longshore Street. Nothing was done to establish a library until January 1877, when a committee was appointed to prepare a circular to secure money and books for a library, as well as to procure a room with lighting fixtures for night reading. On February 6, 1877, the first book was presented to the group along with a gift of $40.50 that was used to purchase 78 books, and the library formerly opened in the school on March 6, 1877. This room served as Tacony's library until January 1, 1880, when the library was moved to the Community Hall and New Era newspaper building on State Road. The Tacony Literary and Library Association then applied for and received a charter from the U.S. Congress. On April 30, 1884, the Keystone Scientific and Literary Association was dissolved and its books transferred to the newly chartered Tacony library. The number of books in the library at the time was 1,284.

When the Henry Disston Saw Works contributed money and promised continued support, the library was renamed the Disston Library and Free Reading Room. Disston rented the third-floor rear room in the Music Hall for the library. With its high ceilings, stately appearance and easy access, it was ideal. In 1893, the number of books in the library had increased to over three thousand, and space in the bank building at Longshore and Tulip Streets was acquired. In 1906, a Carnegie grant was obtained to build a library, and the Mary Disston estate donated land. The library was moved to its current building at Knorr Street and Torresdale Avenue. Again the community turned out and walked the books one pile at a time to the new library.

The only other library in the northeast was the Charles R. King Library adjoining the Chapel of the Redeemer Episcopal Church in Bensalem. It was built in 1882 after Dr. Charles R. King joined the vestry of the All Saints' Episcopal Church on Frankford Avenue in Philadelphia. Born in New York State, Charles was the grandson of Rufus King, New York's representative to the Continental Congress and Constitutional Convention, one of New York's first senators and an ambassador to England during the Washington, Adams and Jefferson administrations. In 1893, Reverend S.F. Hotchkin, writing in his book *The Bristol Pike*, stated that "Dr. Charles King owns the large and fine library of Rufus King, collected by him mainly while ambassador to England. Charles has made many additions to Rufus's collection. This is one of the finest private collections of books in this region."

Charles King designed the library building to be fireproof and fitted to contain one forty- by sixty-square-foot room with bookcases to hold his one-thousand-volume collection. The books were placed there and categorized into the subjects of religion, biography, travel, general literature and standard works of the day. The use of these books was originally restricted to the wealthy of Bensalem/Torresdale, but the library was eventually opened to all and considered a public library. The library is still intact, with many of Charles King's books still there.

Northeast Philadelphia's early efforts that led to the development of libraries came from within each community. Long before any City of Philadelphia initiatives, the Quakers in Byberry and the wealthy, concerned citizens of Torresdale and Holmesburg, along with the industrialists of Tacony and Frankford, had initiated and supported libraries. While the Carnegie grants at the turn of the century were instrumental in the establishment of public libraries in Holmesburg, Tacony and later Frankford, northeast communities were already committed to the idea of having libraries available to all.

Libraries were not the only institutions started in the northeast. Through the efforts of local physician Dr. Benjamin Rush, medical practices and ideas were also being advanced there. He and Thomas Scattergood were responsible for the opening of the Frankford Friends Hospital for the Insane in 1813. This led to Northeast Philadelphia becoming one of the leaders in the nation in the field of treatment for the mentally ill.

***

BENJAMIN RUSH AND THE HEALING HALLS

Among the many unknown but significant stories in the history of Northeast Philadelphia is the important role the area played in the mental health movement in America. For nearly two hundred years, from the late eighteenth century through the late twentieth century, Northeast Philadelphia was a center for ideas and practical treatment of those with mental illness. To understand the history of the mental health movement in the United States, it is crucial to study what took place in Northeast Philadelphia.

It began with Benjamin Rush (1745–1813), whose career as a physician, writer, educator, humanitarian and founding father of the nation makes him one of Northeast Philadelphia's most distinguished citizens. Rush was born in Byberry and spent thirteen of his most prolific years, from 1781 to 1794, in Frankford, where he had a home located on Adams Avenue where Greenwood Cemetery is today. He became involved with mental health when his son John returned home from the navy consumed by guilt after having killed a man in a duel, and soon Rush himself was consumed by guilt. Rush placed John in the mental ward at the hospital, where he eventually died. Rush was appalled at seeing mental patents in chains and cages at the University of Pennsylvania and initiated a successful campaign to build a separate institution for the mentally ill. With the help of his Quaker friend Thomas Scattergood, who was then in England working at the York Retreat—an institution for the mentally ill that practiced a more humane, psychological approach called "moral treatment"—Rush led the fight for reform in the treatment of the mentally ill in Pennsylvania. The issue at hand was clear: while Pennsylvania Hospital, a publicly supported institution, took in mentally ill patients "to keep them off the streets" because they tended to cause "terror among their neighbors," Rush, like the Quakers led by Scattergood, believed that a cure was possible for the mentally ill. Rush served on the medical staff of the Pennsylvania Hospital from 1783 until his death in 1813 and helped to transform its approach to treating mental illness.

In 1813, the Quakers began construction of the Friends Asylum—now Friends Hospital very near Benjamin Rush's former home—in Frankford. It was the first private psychiatric hospital in the United States. The grounds of the hospital were acquired for $120 per acre and covered fifty-eight acres of prime agricultural land, thirty of which was already cultivated. The principal crops were grasses, corn, potatoes and wheat. Six cows supplied the hospital with milk and butter, and a small plot near the kitchen was for vegetables. Even tobacco was grown on the farm but was "restricted to consumption by the convalescent patients." Medical plants, as well as other "salutary" herbs, were also cultivated in large quantities.

But not all of the land was used for farming. The grounds were intended to evoke a feeling of quiet serenity, to make the institution a true "retreat." Broad tree-lined avenues stretched from the public road to the front door of the institution. There were gardens, ponds and a small stream surrounded by other gardens that were rich in variety and color. These amenities were planned and considered part of the hospital's treatment for patients. Much of this humane approach came from Benjamin Rush's 1812 text *Medical Inquiries and Observations upon the Diseases of the Mind*. This publication became the most widely read work on mental illness in the nineteenth century and secured for Rush the title of "Father of American Psychiatry."

Under Rush's plan, cleanliness was seen as an absolute necessity to health. Patients bathed regularly, and attendants made sure that they had clean clothes, linens and rooms. There was to be no more corporal punishment, use of chains or mechanical restraints. In their place were substituted fresh air, gardening, warm baths, exercise and a genuine empathy for the patient. Seclusion in solitary chambers was not to be used unless the patient was judged to be harmful to himself or others. Although Rush died just as work began on Friends Hospital, the institution flourished under his treatment formula. Beautiful gardens, a quiet rural setting and the belief that mental illness was a disease that could be treated soon became the prevailing philosophy of psychiatric institutions. As a result of its success, Friends Hospital became the training ground for future doctors in the field of mental illness.

One such individual was Thomas Story Kirkbride (1809–1883), who was trained to be a surgeon before accepting a position at Friends Hospital in 1832. He would go on to be a towering figure in the field. Kirkbride quickly adapted to the practices used at the Friends Hospital, believing that mental illness was a disease, even to the point of marrying one of his mental patients when his first wife died. Because of his training at Friends Hospital, he was offered the superintendent position at the newly established Pennsylvania Hospital for the Insane at Forty-fourth and Market Streets in 1840. Kirkbride later was a founding member of the Association of Medical Superintendents of American Institutions for the Insane—forerunner of the American Psychiatric Association. His ambition, intellect and strong sense of purpose enabled him to use his stature in the field to become one of the most prominent authorities on mental health care in America during the latter half of the nineteenth century. Kirkbride promoted a standardized method of asylum construction and mental health treatment, popularly known as the "Kirkbride Plan," which significantly influenced both building design and patient treatment practices in America.

An important part of the Kirkbride Plan was to foster moral treatment of mentally ill patients as prescribed by Benjamin Rush. Kirkbride's belief in physical exercise was even stronger than that proposed by Rush and led to the construction of a circular railroad at Friends Hospital as early as 1837. This was just one of his ideas to keep patients active and engaged while having fun. The railroad car was actually a small vehicle equipped with pedals that was propelled

Picture of Frankford Friends Hospital with its railroad exercise car constructed for the use by patients from 1830 to 1880.

like a bicycle around a tract in front of the main building. The railway was still there in 1889 when the hospital added to the exercise program by building the first gymnasium in America.

Rush's and Kirkbride's programs became the standard treatments for the mentally ill in nineteenth-century America. They had established many of the basic principles that would become part of modern-day mental care. But the public clamor during the Victorian age to get "crazy people off the streets" promoted a whole new direction for the mental health movement in the early years of the twentieth century. Reform recommendations now included building sizable state-run institutions that could house and treat large numbers of patients at the same time. Again, Northeast Philadelphia became a center for the implementation of these new ideas.

***

SLAVE, FREEDOM AND CITIZENSHIP

A common misconception among Philadelphians is that Northeast Philadelphia is the white section of the city and has always been that way. Nothing could be further from the truth. There has always been a significant African American presence in the northeast, and slavery was an early institution introduced by traders to the area. A trip to the Trinity Oxford Church graveyard near Burholme, where there is a cluster of early seventeenth-century graves marked by the first names of slaves, attests to the fact that there were blacks in Northeast Philadelphia very early in its settlement. The practice of burying blacks and whites together was very unusual at the time, but it does indicate the close association between the races in remote regions like far Northeast Philadelphia, which was a thinly populated rural area in the 1700s. There were notices in newspapers of slave sales and runaway slaves in Frankford in the 1740s and references to African Americans in official records and in diaries of Frankford residents in the eighteenth century. The recent discovery of the Holme family papers shows that there were slaves working as handymen and domestics at the family homestead,

Box Grove, in Holmesburg. It is clear from these early records that there were only one or two slaves per family and that they were usually field hands or household servants. Many stayed with the families and worked for them after being freed. When slaves were gradually emancipated by Pennsylvania law in 1780, some of these freed African Americans settled in the section of Holmesburg where the Mount Zion Baptist church is today.

Also quite common in that period was the marriage of free African Americans to Indians of the Leni-Lenape tribe. There were many such mixed marriages, but the most widely known in early Northeast Philadelphia was that of Cyrus Bustill, an African American baker from Bustleton. Honored and remembered for his gift of freshly baked bread for George Washington's army during the Revolution, Bustill was known throughout Bustleton and Byberry. His marriage to an Indian woman initiated a family of black activists in Philadelphia for the next one hundred years. Throughout the years of racial riots and civil rights struggles, a Bustill descendant usually found his way into the limelight.

It is evident from the federal census that slavery died a slow death in Pennsylvania. The 1810 census indicates that there were 795 slaves in the state. By 1830, the number had decreased to 403, and in 1840, the last census that listed slaves, the number had decreased to 64. As slaves became free, they tended to move into their own houses and neighborhoods while continuing to do the work they had previously done. Many freed slaves moved into Frankford, where there was work and support from a sizable black community that had existed since the very early 1800s.

By the mid-nineteenth century, there were three significant communities of African Americans in Northeast Philadelphia: Frankford, Holmesburg and Byberry. The largest, Frankford, was centered near Plum, Meadow and Foulkrod Streets around Campbell AME Church. Composed of blacks who were servants in the homes of whites or who had been farm laborers, these African Americans soon became independent of whites. By 1850, half the black population of Frankford lived in homes that they owned. They formed the backbone of the brick-making industry, and some were being hired at the time to work for James Horrocks in his factory, one of the few white industries to hire blacks. The Frankford African American community was large enough that it developed its own network of shopkeepers, tradesman, horsemen and mule men.

The Bethany AME above Holme Circle is the oldest black church in Northeast Philadelphia. This area was once called Guinea Hill, and much of the nearby land belonged to blacks. The gravestone of Richard C. Stout (1884–1958) is located here.

In the second-largest African American community in the northeast, Holmesburg, most blacks were servants in wealthy white homes, but an increasing number began to work in the grain mills along Pennypack Creek. This black community was not as large as that of Frankford and did not develop its own system of shops and tradesman, so its members had to buy their food and supplies from whites. This promoted a closer relationship between the races in Holmesburg—to the point where black and white children played together. In fact, black and white children attended the early J.H. Brown School together, while blacks in Frankford attended the all-black Wilmont School. Smaller African American populations in the northeast tended to promote schools that allowed the races to be educated together because there were insufficient funds to afford a separate school for blacks.

The third area in the northeast that had a significant African American population in the nineteenth century was Byberry. In this region, far from the city, African Americans with money could buy farms cheaply and operate them. Although the black community in Byberry was very small, it was significant because the strong Quaker presence permitted an active abolitionist movement to develop there. In the 1840s, black activist Robert Purvis built Byberry Hall specifically to house abolitionist meetings. Men like William Lloyd Garrison and other nationally known abolitionist were frequent visitors to Byberry, where they formulated plans for the national abolitionist movement. Thus, Byberry was widely recognized for its antislavery sentiments even though its African American population was never large. Most blacks had left the area by 1900, but many of the buildings from the abolitionist era remain clustered around Byberry Friends Meetinghouse.

Somewhat disconnected from the other black communities of Northeast Philadelphia was the African American population of Tacony. When World War I began in 1918 the men from Tacony enlisted en masse into a hospital-ambulance unit that was sent off to the battlefields of France. This left the Disston Saw Works, the major employer of the area, short of workers. The Pennsylvania Railroad, to meet wartime demands for labor, carried blacks north from Virginia free of charge. William D. Disston, then president of Disston Saw, offered to do the same. Sending company representatives Harry and Edmund Whittaker to Remington and Rice, Virginia, William was able to entice four hundred black workers from that area to come to Tacony. Some were given housing on Wissinoming Street, then

Star of Hope Baptist Church in Tacony in 1919. These blacks were brought to Tacony in boxcars to work at the Disston Saw factory during World War I.

owned by the Mary Disston estate and dubbed the "Mary Seven." Others lived out of jerry-rigged boxcars set off on the railroad siding at State Road between Cottman and Princeton Avenues. These lodgings were assigned by the Disston Company. A married man with a family was given at low cost a house on Wissinoming Street, while unmarried men slept in the boxcars with portable bathroom facilities. The arrangement worked well for Disston but not so well for the black workers, who lost their jobs to the returning servicemen when the war ended in November 1919. A small percentage of the transplanted blacks were asked to continue working at Disston, but most were let go. Many moved to Frankford seeking work, and a few returned to Remington, but some stayed to form a black community in Tacony. They settled along Wissinoming Street in the area east of State Road, opened the Star of Hope Baptist Church south of Cottman Avenue and sent their children to Hamilton Disston School like the rest of Tacony. But like the Italians who lived nearby, these blacks were marginal to Tacony's social life. Isolated and economically disadvantaged, both groups suffered the consequences of being on the wrong side of the tracks in this small town with its predominantly English culture. By 1921, the Tacony African American community had declined to about twenty houses. The final hardship came to the community in the 1950s when Wissinoming Street was taken by the city for the building of I-95.

This brief survey of the African American communities in the early years of Northeast Philadelphia history demonstrates that they've been part of the northeast for hundreds of years. Many blacks in Holmesburg and Frankford can trace their family histories back to colonial days.

CHAPTER 2

A GILDED TRANSFORMATION

From Summer Retreat to Bustling Center

***

TORRESDALE IN THE DAYS OF RISDON'S FERRY

As the population grew, the northeast region of Philadelphia became known for its farms and summer vacation homes owned by wealthy families from the city. Individuals played a large role in what happened in Torresdale. This formed the backdrop for the events that were about to happen between 1850 and 1900. While often neglected by historians, the lifestyles in this section remain physically connected to other parts of the northeast yet developed entirely differently. Because Torresdale was so different from the traditional farming communities around it, the contrast presents a different view to the conventional ideas about Northeast Philadelphia. Torresdale remains today a unique part of the region.

In the early 1800s, Northeast Philadelphia consisted of underdeveloped open space and large, isolated farm holdings interspersed with a few small villages like Holmesburg, Five Points (now Burholme), Bustleton, Byberry and Risdon's Ferry (now Torresdale). Most of these villages were connected to the larger commercial town of Frankford by dirt roads. The most heavily traveled of these roads were Bristol Pike, Oxford Pike and

Bustleton Pike. They were called "pikes" because they were toll roads on which a gatekeeper turned a large wooden pike to let travelers through at certain points along the road. Risdon's Ferry area was named after John Risdon, owner of a hotel and ferry on the Delaware River just south of the Poquessing Creek. Originally, Risdon operated the ferry for travelers heading to New Jersey by way of the Rancocas River. It often carried passengers as far east as Mount Holly, making for convenient travel between Northeast Philadelphia and parts of New Jersey. The existence of the ferry accounts for the extension of roads like Academy Road and Grant Avenue to the Delaware River early in the nineteenth century. Risdon made enough money from his ferry business to build a hotel for use by travelers in this period.

The development of the steamboat by Robert Fulton on the Hudson River in the early nineteenth century would forever change commerce in the Risdon's Ferry area. By 1820, the first steamboat line began operation on the Delaware River between Philadelphia and Trenton. In the northeast part of the city there were three daily stops: Bridesburg/Frankford, Tacony/Holmesburg and Risdon's Ferry. Due to its strategic location, Risdon's Ferry became the focal point for commerce in far Northeast Philadelphia and lower Bensalem Township in Bucks County. Since there was no wharf, the passengers were transferred to shore by small boats. The area had previously been called Poquessing, after the Native American name for the creek meaning "mice"—they found it overrun with muskrats. As commercial activity increased on the river, Risdon's Ferry became the most commonly used name for the area.

By the 1840s, Risdon's Ferry had developed into one of the population centers of Northeast Philadelphia. Even today, as one travels on Fitler and Milnor Streets between State Road and the river, one can see the houses, even some brownstones built in the 1840s, from the early town of Risdon's Ferry. Many of the town's residents were workers at the hotel, its many stables or the ferry. They helped with the U.S. Mail station that handled the mail dropped off each day for the upper northeast and parts of Bensalem. The town was full of people waiting on horseback for their mail, waiting to ride the ferry to New Jersey or waiting to take the steamship to Philadelphia. Before William H. Gatzmer's Tacony to Trenton Railroad began operation in 1846, the steamboat at Risdon's Ferry was the only means of fast transportation to the city and for locals to get their mail. This resulted in the establishment of many stables in the town at which horses could be housed and cared for as people traveled.

A Gilded Transformation

The steamship *Twilight*, constructed in 1869, carried passengers daily from Risdon's Ferry to center city Philadelphia until it was taken out of service in the 1920s.

Many Northeast Philadelphia residents took the steamboat every morning at 8:00 a.m. from Risdon's Ferry to Market Street, did their work or shopping in center city and then took the 3:00 p.m. boat back, having tea on the deck on their way back home. The trip usually took one hour. Young women from Philadelphia's best families were drawn to this vacation spot because of the large number of eligible young bachelors from the city enjoying outings there. People of wealth in the city, both old and young, soon discovered this Garden of Eden along the river on the outskirts of the city. Risdon established a hotel near his boat dock to be used for overnight stays by people from the city. What a delight for them to take in the peaceful sight of boats on the Delaware or the beautiful sunsets over the forests of New Jersey. There was also plenty for them to do: playing cards for money at the casino, renting a horse and riding through the beautiful countryside that is today Torresdale or going fishing for shad in the fish-laden Delaware River.

This lifestyle became part of the customs and culture of the Victorian age for wealthy Philadelphians. Men of fortune, seeking relief from the hot and stressful workdays in the city, chose the cool banks of the Delaware River as a retreat. Eventually, the wealthiest families began building mansions along the river in the areas near Risdon's Ferry.

A picture from the Delaware River of the Morelton Inn vacation spot for the rich visitors from Philadelphia. This became the summer vacation spot in Torresdale on the Delaware River beginning in the 1840s.

Charles Macalester, a Philadelphia financier of Scottish descent, bought the entire area from John Risdon, including Morelton Hotel in 1850. Risdon retired to Holmesburg, where he owned the Washington Hotel on Bristol Pike and maintained a stage line between Holmesburg and Philadelphia. His daughter Elizabeth married Jonathan Rowland of the Rowland Shovel Works. Risdon then became active in activities in Holmesburg.

Macalester not only purchased Risdon's Ferry but also the most northeasterly part of the city then called Poquessing. Macalester was a frequent visitor to William Biddle's estate in Andalusia two miles up the river since it now bordered on his vast landholdings. Macalester lived in Risdon's hotel while his magnificent estate was being built on the south side of the confluence of the Poquessing Creek and Delaware River. He renamed the area Torresdale, in honor of his old hunting lodge (Torrisdale) in Scotland. Once his home was completed, he called it Glengarry, after the family estate in the highlands of Scotland. The property would later be purchased by Robert Foerderer, who would combine two family names and call the estate Glen Foerd. Edward Hopkins, Macalester's brother-in-law, bought Risdon's old hotel from Macalester and had it demolished, replacing it with a brownstone mansion known as the Morelton Inn. This was to become a gathering place for the rich and famous of Philadelphia for the next four decades.

Hopkins saw his clientele grow to include families such as Drexel, Foerderer, Fitler, Morrell, Middleton, Phillips, Borie, Brown and Biddle. Many of these families would build mansions and live in the area. Local churches were well suited for these families. The All Saints' Episcopal Church on Frankford Avenue south of Grant Avenue had been in existence since 1772, and Eden Hall Chapel and St. Dominic's Catholic Church, since 1849. (The latter was where the Drexel family attended services.) These churches were used in the summertime by the rich who came to Torresdale to escape the heat of the city.

Activities at the Morelton Hotel for guests in the late 1800s consisted of early morning or evening boat trips by gentlemen, which included afternoon tea service, concerts overlooking the river, tennis courts, vast gardens with pathways, a racetrack near the Morrell estate and a nearby casino operated especially for hotel guests. Some gentlemen would venture to the Torresdale Golf Club, founded in 1896, or to what is now Mud Island to shoot quail. A secret held by all at the time was that a brothel operated on the upper floors of the casino. As was the case wherever the rich played and gathered, they knew how to live well.

One thing is clear from this early history of Torresdale. Along with the more famous Philadelphia mainline, Torresdale had been the city's posh suburban neighborhood of the late 1800s and early 1900s. A visit to the houses in the original Risdon's Ferry neighborhood gives us a glimpse of the area's former grandeur and lifestyle. As one gazes at the Delaware River with its opening into the Rancocas River on the New Jersey side, it is easy to understand the significance of this location to the early commerce of the region.

***

SAINT AND PIONEER: KATHARINE MARY DREXEL

For many of the rich people who owned summer homes there in the eighteen and nineteenth centuries, Torresdale was a place for solitude and contemplation of a life to be lived. Katharine Mary Drexel, daughter of Francis Anthony Drexel, president of an international

The official portrait of Mother Drexel after she assumed the leadership of the Sisters of the Blessed Sacrament.

banking empire based in Philadelphia and partner with J.P. Morgan, was no exception. Born in November 26, 1858, Katharine was the second daughter of Francis and Hanna Langstroth Drexel, Hanna having given birth to Katharine's sister, Elizabeth, three years earlier. Hanna died five weeks after Katharine's birth, however. Two years later, Francis married Emma M. Bouvier, an ancestor of Jacqueline Bouvier Kennedy. Louise, Katharine's half-sister, was born from this marriage. The three sisters remained close the rest of their lives. Despite being members of Philadelphia's high society, Francis and Emma Drexel were generous and unstinting in their support of charitable causes. While Francis was in his office making unbelievable sums of money, Emma was at home giving generous portions of it to the poor and needy.

The Drexel family residence was officially a mansion at 1503 Walnut Street in downtown Philadelphia, but the family's real love was their summer home in Torresdale. The property possessed beautiful gardens, sloping lawns, a variety of flowering trees and an atmosphere of quiet beauty. It was here that Katharine formulated her life's mission, which eventually led to her work in the Catholic Church. In addition to spending their summers in Torresdale, the Drexels, like many rich Philadelphians, often traveled throughout Europe. But the exquisite and beautiful sights found there had little interest for young Katharine. To her "they were like a big, beautiful doll filled with sawdust." The family also took a trip to the western United States when Katharine was young, where she saw firsthand the poverty and destitution of the Native American population.

In her twenties, Katharine was courted by Prince George, heir to the British Crown, during a Cape May, New Jersey vacation. Hearing this, her father wrote Katharine that "many a man with a title would do anything to join their nobility to the legendary wealth of an American heiress." Francis then went on to warn her: "Don't let them steal away your heart." Katharine's character was being formed during these early years by her family's habits and values. Most contemplation and discussion of the meaning of life took place at the Nest, the name the Drexel family gave to their home in Torresdale. Katharine, with her sister Elizabeth and stepsister Louise, felt most comfortable there and most freely able to have these open discussions. The family also enjoyed their nearby friends and neighbors in Torresdale and were well liked throughout the

Drexel family home, San Michel, in Torresdale, with an unidentified woman standing in front of the house. *Courtesy of the Archives of the Sisters of the Blessed Sacrament.*

neighborhood. In fact, in 1889, Louise Drexel would marry family friend Colonel Edward Morrell, a prominent Torresdale lawyer and landholder (Morrell Park is named after him).

Katharine lost her father and stepmother in the years 1883 and 1885, respectively. Francis's will, like his life, was a masterpiece of helping the poor. He bequeathed over $1 million to charity and a trust fund of $14 million to be divided equally among his three daughters. Local newspapers announced at the time that each of the Drexel girls would receive the unbelievable sum of $1,000 per day for their lifetimes.

Shortly after Francis's death, two Catholic missionaries visited the Drexel sisters in Philadelphia. The missionaries had spent a lifetime working with the Indians of the West. Katharine, having seen for herself the awful plight of the Native Americans and having recently read Helen Hunt Jackson's book *A Century of Dishonor*, a woeful history of Indian-white relations in the United States, promised to help their cause. This prompted a visit with Bishop James O'Connor of Omaha, Nebraska. Bishop O'Connor had been pastor of St. Dominic's Church in Holmesburg in the 1870s and had been a friend and spiritual advisor to Katharine. They met in the Dakotas, where a meeting was arranged with Red Cloud, the famous Sioux Indian chief. This strengthened Katharine's interest in helping Native Americans. She returned to Torresdale and set up the first systematic financing of Indian missionaries in the western states.

To lighten the burden of sorrow the three girls felt from the loss of their parents, an extensive tour of Europe was planned in 1887. While in Rome, the sisters were granted two private audiences with Pope Leo XIII. Katharine had been contemplating a religious life since she was thirteen, but now it was becoming something she seriously considered. During her meeting with the pope, Katharine requested that he send more missionaries to help the American Indians. The pope responded by asking, "Why my child, don't you yourself become a missionary?"

This question led to a lengthy correspondence with her old friend from St. Dominic's, Bishop James O'Connor. As Katharine formulated her plans with O'Connor, a February 1889 letter from him challenged her to act: "You have decided to become a Religious. The next thing for you to determine is whether you shall establish a new order in the church for Indians and Colored people." Katharine was not enthused by the idea, stating, "The responsibility of such a calling almost crushes me, because I am so definitely poor in the virtues necessary."

The bishop refused to hear her doubts and arranged for her religious training with the Sisters of Mercy in Pittsburgh. When Katharine went to the Pittsburgh convent in early 1889, the *Philadelphia Public Ledger* announced in a headline, "Miss Drexel Enters a Catholic Convent: Gives up Seven Million Dollars." She completed her training in eight months and was ordained into the Sisters of Mercy in November 1889. However, disappointment followed when her friend and advisor Bishop O'Connor died on May 27, 1890. Hearing of Katharine's grief and loss, Archbishop Patrick J. Ryan of Philadelphia visited her in Torresdale. He offered help. "If I share the burden with you, if I help you, can you go on?" She answered with a simple, "Yes."

Katharine's sister Elizabeth and her husband Walter George Smith (1854–1924) arrived home from a lengthy European honeymoon on September 7, 1890. Three weeks later, after giving premature birth to a child, Elizabeth died. During one of the largest funerals ever held in Northeast Philadelphia, Katharine knelt before the casket in front of a crowd of hundreds of Torresdale and Holmesburg residents at her Torresdale summer home. To Katharine, Elizabeth seemed so young and the child in her arms too tiny to be there.

The death of Elizabeth sharpened Katharine's already clear perspective on life. Nothing of her vast Drexel fortune could relieve Elizabeth's pain or prevent her death. This forced Katharine to question the meaning of wealth, power and prestige, as well as her life's meaning. She knew that becoming a nun and establishing an order for African Americans and Native Americans was her real calling.

On February 12, 1891, Katharine Drexel professed her vows as the first Sister of the Blessed Sacrament for Indians and Colored People in America. To the usual vows of poverty, chastity and obedience she added a fourth: "To be the mother and servant of the Indian and Negro races according to the rule of the Sisters of the Blessed Sacrament; and not to undertake any work which would lead to the neglect or abandonment of the Indian and Colored races."

She opened her Torresdale home to the Sisters of the Blessed Sacrament, establishing the Divine Holy Providence School, a boarding school for the poor children of Holmesburg and Torresdale. She purchased a tract of land in the Cornwell Heights section of Bensalem on which she would build a school and mother house for her order. She consulted her brother-in-law Colonel Morrell on legal and financial matters concerning the construction of these buildings.

A constant procession of visitors came to Torresdale and later to Cornwell Heights seeking help for blacks and Indians. The opening of Indian schools in Texas, the Dakotas and across the West followed. Then there were schools for blacks founded in Virginia and Alabama. Staffed by Sisters of the Blessed Sacrament who had been trained in Northeast Philadelphia, Katharine Drexel's new order was having a significant influence on America's relationships with Africans and Native Americans. By 1942, she and her order had established a system of black Catholic schools in thirteen states, with thirty convents, forty missions and twenty-three rural schools in which fifteen thousand children were educated. Even more important than money and institutions, Katharine Drexel had awakened in America a moral and religious outrage against the unfair treatment of Indians and blacks. This would be her lasting gift to her country.

Katharine Drexel died on May 3, 1955, in Bensalem, Pennsylvania, at the age of ninety-six. The most fitting tribute to her appeared in Philadelphia newspapers at the time of her death. "One of the most remarkable women in the history of America was called home yesterday…She belongs so truly to all America, but especially to the poor and forgotten people of the land—our Indians and Negroes. She was indeed a heroine."

Katharine Drexel was canonized a saint by the Catholic Church in 1988. She is buried at Sisters of the Blessed Sacrament Mother House in Cornwell Heights, where there is a shrine to her that is visited by thousands of people annually. The Drexel estate in Torresdale is now part of the Torresdale campus of Frankford Hospital. Both the family home and chapel are still standing and part of the hospital complex.

✳✳✳

TORRESDALE: HOME OF THE CREAM OF PHILADELPHIA SOCIETY

As described earlier, the Risdon's Ferry area across from the Rancocas Creek in New Jersey was the nucleus of what would become Torresdale. Prior to 1860, this area began to develop into the preferred community for many of Philadelphia's wealthy families. Most of the early landowners built large mansions with wealth garnered from their work in Philadelphia's financial industry. Among these early families were the Biddles, Macalesters, Drexels and Morrells. Their influence on the development of Torresdale would span the next one hundred years.

Nicholas Biddle (1786–1844) lived in Andalusia above the Poquessing Creek but spent much of his time in the home of friends in Torresdale. As president of the Second Bank of America under President Andrew Jackson, he was a very powerful figure in his day. Charles Macalester, who worked in Biddle's bank, was a trusted friend of Presidents Jackson, Van Buren, Polk, Fillmore, Pierce, Buchanan, Lincoln and Grant. Macalester later became director of the Fidelity Trust and Safe Deposit Company, where he brokered many of Philadelphia's most famous corporation deals. Francis Drexel (1824–1885) went to work at his father's banking house as a lad and with his brother Anthony built Drexel and Company into one of the nation's most powerful financial institutions. Colonel Edward Morrell (1864–1896) was the grandson of Colonel Louis de Tousard, author of a French military text on artillery and a friend of General Lafayette. From the time of his birth, Morrell was perceived by those around him to be a military man. He was elected select councilman for Philadelphia's thirty-fifth ward and then appointed by the governor of Pennsylvania to command the Third Regiment of the Pennsylvania National Guard. Morrell also was president of the Upper Delaware Transportation Company and a director of the Bourse, the commodities exchange corporation of Philadelphia. Unlike any other community in Northeast Philadelphia, Torresdale became a community that had a lifestyle that reflected its status as a home for the rich and powerful people of the city.

The heyday for Torresdale would come with the generation of rich men who moved into the area after the Civil War. As opposed to members of earlier generations who were mainly financiers, these later families were composed of newly rich Philadelphia manufacturers. These families would marry into the earlier, wealthy families to initiate a new upper-class elite in Torresdale. Prominent among these manufacturing families were the Foerderers, Smiths, Bories, Morrells, Fitlers, Browns, Grants, Pearsons, Dolans and Masseys. Each relied on a factory to provide the resources to support the family's Torresdale mansion. Robert Foerderer's (1860–1903) leather plant in Frankford employed nearly one thousand men and allowed him time to travel

The famous racetrack used by the rich and famous of Torresdale, located on the northwest corner of Red Lion and Knights Roads. Notice in the picture that all in attendance are well dressed—no farmers came to these sulky races in Torresdale. People in attendance were guests of the wealthy families of Torresdale or stayed at the Morelton Inn. Edward Morrell raced his best horses on this track. *Courtesy of the Archives of the Sisters of Blessed Sacrament.*

the globe looking for quality furs. In 1873, Foerderer purchased Macalester's mansion and renamed it Glen Foerd.

Thomas Kilby Smith (1820–1887) was Ulysses S. Grant's acting chief of staff during the Civil War, commanding a brigade at Shiloh. He also commanded a regiment in General Sherman's Atlanta campaign. These associations won him high esteem and respect after the war. He later served as U.S. consul to Panama during negotiations on a treaty for the canal. His son Walter George Smith (1854–1924), an author and writer for the *Catholic Encyclopedia*, married Francis Drexel's daughter Elizabeth and lived with her on the corner of Fitler and Milnor Streets until her death in 1890. Walter traveled extensively and had considerable influence with the Vatican. The Torresdale mansions were rarely without an international guest, whose visit was arranged by Walter Smith. He and Elizabeth continually purchased land in Torresdale, giving them much influence in the region.

Thomas Dolan, who controlled much of the city's textile industry through his ownership of the Keystone Kitting Mills, was described as the richest business "tycoon" in Philadelphia.

Edwin H. Fitler (1825–1896), mayor of Philadelphia from 1887 to 1871, owned a mansion next to Morelton Inn on Milnor Street. His wealth came from his rope factory in Wissinoming.

Others were equally prominent. Samuel Grant was a medical drug producer (Grant Avenue is named after him); Isaac Pearson was a horsewhip manufacturer; brothers Adolph and Charles Borie acquired wealth in the shipping trade (Adolph later became secretary of the navy in President Grant's administration); and Nelson Brown, known in Torresdale for his famous "tally-ho" hunting call, retired from a manufacturing career to become a Torresdale favorite. The famous Northeast Horse Show Parades of the 1930s held at Welsh Road and Roosevelt Boulevard reenacted the Nelson Brown tradition by having the "Tally-Ho" wagon lead the parade and open the event.

Everyone in Torresdale knew Henry V. Massey, even though he was not really part of the wealthy class. He was educated in Philadelphia public schools, graduated from Central High and went on to get his law degree at the University of Pennsylvania. Massey was an aggressive lawyer who recognized and took advantage of local opportunities to become one of the most influential men of Torresdale. He held numerous local board positions, including secretary and treasurer of the Bristol Turnpike Company, director of the Suburban Electric Company in Tacony,

A Gilded Transformation

Morrell family and friends ride down Frankford Avenue in their four-horse Tally-Ho coach in Torresdale. *Courtesy of the Archives of the Sisters of the Blessed Sacrament.*

director of the Tacony Trust Company, director of Holmesburg Water Company and a trustee of the Lower Dublin Academy. In Torresdale, Massey was the vice-president of the Upper Delaware Transportation Company and on the boards of the Morelton Inn Company and the Torresdale Land Improvement Company. His estate, which was farm-like and not a mansion, was located on the southeast corner of Grant and Frankford Avenues.

Although Massey lacked the background and money to be part of the Torresdale elite, he was welcomed into their homes and parties. Since many of these families owned shares in local ventures, they were comfortable having someone from the community like Massey run their daily affairs. When a problem or need arose, Massey was the one to get things done.

The heart of the Torresdale community at the time was the Morelton Inn at Fitler Street and the river. It attracted large crowds in the summer and paid a handsome return on investments. Electric lighting had become America's new fascination in the 1890s following Nikola Telsa's electrical demonstrations in New York and Philadelphia. While there was a small electrical station in Tacony used by the Disston Saw company, there was no electricity beyond that point. The residents of Torresdale knew that an electrically illuminated Morelton Inn, with its lights twinkling on the river at night, would make it the most attractive spot on the river. To get this done they turned to Massey. Using his connections on the various boards on which he served, he arranged for a separate electrical line to be run from Tacony to the Morelton, making it the only electrically lit house and garden in Torresdale until Edward Morrell installed his generator. Visitors to Torresdale marveled at the sight of the beauty of the Morelton Inn at night, making the decades at the turn of the century some of the most memorable in Torresdale history.

One of the highest-profile social events in Torresdale history occurred in 1894 when the Rowing Association of American Colleges held its annual regatta at the Morelton Inn site on the Delaware. For one weekend, crews from Harvard, Yale, University of Pennsylvania and other elite colleges lived it up in Torresdale, enjoying the casino and brothel available there at the time. It was decided by an embarrassed Torresdale community not to host this National College Regatta again.

The forces that eventually changed the face of Torresdale began in 1909 when Philadelphia decided to improve its municipal water supply. For years the high death rate of children in the city had been known to be directly related to its inadequate water system. Much of the problem was in Kensington, where water intake pipes were located too close to city wastewater pipes. New flush toilet systems that came into widespread use in this period further complicated the issue since they were directly connected to the wastewater pipes. The solution was to build a water supply plant far up the Delaware to provide the city with clean water. The best location was determined to be along the river in Torresdale, across from the Rancocas Creek, where the flow of clean water was at its maximum.

The selection of that area by city officials had a great impact on the wealthy people who lived along the river in Torresdale. Once construction began on the water works, the area was inundated by hundreds of laborers, loud noise, dust and smells. One can visit the Samuel Baxter Water Plant at State Road and Linden Avenue to appreciate what the size and scope of this 1909 project must have been. To those accustomed to the peace and quiet of Torresdale, it was as if the city had moved into the neighborhood.

Another factor that led to the movement of the wealthy elite out of Torresdale in the early twentieth century was the rising popularity

City officials stand in a large water main in Torresdale that was to carry water to the
Lardner's Point water pumping station in Tacony and then be pumped to the entire city.

of the newly invented automobile. This new form of transportation
opened up areas that did not rely on the river for easy access. It
became common for wealthy families to drive to the New Jersey shore
and enjoy its beaches and natural beauty. Vacation homes for such
families were now being built in places like Atlantic City and Ocean
City instead of Torresdale. An example of this was the spacious John
B. Kelly vacation home in Ocean City. Some wealthy families did
continue to live in Torresdale, but their lifestyle now represented that
from another generation.

Other changes soon took place in the community of Torresdale. The
Delaware Yacht Club opened in 1926 on Milnor Street in the center of
the wealthiest section of Torresdale. It was not founded by the rich and
famous of Philadelphia but by people interested in sailing. Early charter
records indicate that the founders were hardworking family members
from Tacony, Holmesburg and Olney. They banded together to purchase
two 1840 brownstone houses for a clubhouse. While some of the richer
families have been members of the club, it is clear that the club has
always had strong representation from hardworking middle-class people
who love boating and enjoy riding in boats on the river.

Change had come to Torresdale by the 1930s. The construction of Roosevelt Boulevard, Samuel Baxter Water Plant, the Frankford El and the Tacony-Palmyra Bridge from the 1900s to the 1920s made Torresdale more accessible and opened up even more opportunities for housing developments. Many of the grand old estates were sold off and divided up for housing lots. In the post–World War II period, Torresdale would experience explosive growth, like many other Northeast Philadelphia communities.

Despite these changes, vestiges of Torresdale's former grandeur can be seen in such surviving buildings as Macalester's Glen Foerd and the estates of Henry Massey, Francis Drexel, T. Kilby Smith, William Biddle and Charles R. King. The Drexel home and chapel, like many of these homes, can still be seen today at the Frankford-Torresdale Hospital complex.

***

SOCIALITE COLONEL EDWARD MORRELL

People living in Morrell Park in Northeast Philadelphia have little idea how the area received its name. Morrell Park is situated on what was a three-hundred-acre country farm purchased in 1888 by a young lawyer named Colonel Edward Morrell. Morrell married Louise Drexel, the youngest daughter of financial wizard Francis Drexel, the same year. Both Edward and Louise loved their summer place in Torresdale and lived there for the remainder of their lives. The Morrells were among the most admired and recognized members of the Torresdale community until their deaths—Colonel Edward Morrell in 1917 and Louise Drexel Morrell in 1945. The life of Louise Morrell has often been described in accounts of her half-sister Katharine Drexel, a saint in the Catholic Church, but little has ever been written about Colonel Edward Morrell, for whom Morrell Park is named.

Edward Morrell was born in 1863, eldest son of Dr. Edward Morrell and Ida Powel. His great-grandfather was Colonel Louis de Tousard, author of the standard manual on artillery practices, commandant of the United States artillery and a friend of the esteemed French general,

Colonel Edward Morrell on horseback in command of the Third Pennsylvania militia unit. *Courtesy of the Archives of the Sisters of the Blessed Sacrament.*

the Marquis de Lafayette. On the day of Edward's birth, the members of the Powel family, who are known today because they founded Powelton Village in west Philadelphia, proudly announced that another military man had been born into the family. The Civil War had just begun, and military matters were the mode of the day. Therefore, it was not hard for the family to believe that Edward Morrell was destined to follow in his great-grandfather's footsteps to military glory. His military bearing made people comfortable, so they called him Colonel Morrell even though he never served a day in the United States military.

In 1870, when Edward was seven years old, his father died, heartbroken over losing the family fortune by investing in a failed sugar plantation in Cuba. Edward was ten years old when his mother remarried John G. Johnson, a lawyer who was handling the Morrell estate in court. Johnson was not the usual attorney of the day. The *New York Times* in 1917 referred to Johnson as the "greatest lawyer in the English speaking world."

Johnson treated his new son like he was his own. The word "stepchild" was never used in the home. Letters between them always began with "My Son or Dearest Dad." John G. Johnson was proud of his son and carefully supervised his education. This relationship directed Edward

Morrell to the University of Pennsylvania so he could follow in his father's footsteps. An outstanding student at Pennsylvania, he was invited to give the graduation speech for his class at the 1883 commencement exercises. His famous father, who was at the time being considered for a justice position on the Supreme Court, was in the audience, having chosen his son's topic: "Constitutional Restraints upon the Uncontrollable Powers of the Majority." It was expected by all that Edward Morrell would join his father's law firm after graduation to begin his apprenticeship, which he did.

Once he began working at his father's law firm, a number of things became clear. Although he was exceedingly bright and forceful in his beliefs, he was not a workaholic like his father. He was very much his mother's son. He easily made friends and was a social gadfly well known in the wealthy social circles of the city. When and where he met Louise Drexel is unclear, but he was attracted to her and to the Drexel family, all of whom called him by his nickname "Ned."

Young Edward Morrell had already acquired the tastes and habits of a true aristocrat. A 1947 *Philadelphia Record* column described Morrell in the 1880s as "the handsomest man in town with dark hair and long, rakish moustache...all of the girls wanted to marry him." He chose Louise Drexel, who had the immense wealth and beauty to complement his taste. Louise, on the other hand, had more serious issues. Edward Morrell was Protestant and she a devout Catholic and very close to her sisters, whom she loved dearly and wanted to live near. So Louise refused Edward's first offer of marriage. But Edward was persistent, converting to Catholicism and agreeing to purchase a Torresdale farm from Simon Cannell only a walking distance from San Michel, the Drexel summer home. With these new arrangements in place, Louise and Edward wed in one of Philadelphia's largest weddings at the Cathedral of Saint Peter and Paul on January 17, 1889. Following the ceremony, the happy couple departed for a honeymoon in the Southwest and Mexico. Returning home, the Morrells named their new summer home San Jose in memory of their trip.

After their marriage, the Morrells kept magnificent homes in Philadelphia's Rittenhouse Square and in Torresdale (San Jose), as well as in Newport, Rhode Island. A convivial man, Morrell continued his membership in the thirteen smartest clubs in the city, kept show horses at San Jose and maintained a handsome "coach and four" Tally-Ho carriages that participated in many parades in Philadelphia and New

York well into the age of the automobile. No society dance in Torresdale would start without Edward Morrell leading the way.

Edward Morrell was very active in Republican Party politics in the city. In 1882, he served as a member of the select council of the thirty-fifth ward in Northeast Philadelphia, then as a member of the city council representing Northeast Philadelphia and, finally, as a state representative from Northeast Philadelphia. In 1900, he was appointed to fill an unexpired term in Congress and was reelected three times from the Fifth Pennsylvania District, serving until 1907. As a member of Congress, Morrell vigorously promoted the rights of Native Americans and African Americans and was of invaluable help to Katharine Drexel's causes. In 1904, the question was raised by the southern states as to the possibility of removing the Fourteenth and Fifteenth Amendments from the Constitution so that Negroes could no longer vote. It was Edward Morrell who led the fight against it. He simply stated that "the Negro is now free and is equal of the white man in respecting to civil and political rights and it should remain so." Still, in Morrell's manuscript collection is a letter from the Tuskegee Normal School written by Booker T. Washington admiring his actions: "Your wise and statesmanlike remarks in Congress will do much to aid the cause of my people."

Morrell was always interested in bettering conditions in Torresdale and improving San Jose, his country estate. The Morrells often purchased land in Torresdale just to keep it up or improve it. Edward Morrell considered highways a mark of a civilized society; using his own money, he had the roads near his home telfordized (hard surfaced). An early advocate of electricity, he had a power plant built on his grounds to provide for lighted areas at San Jose. Morrell's greatest love at San Jose was his horses. He was well known throughout Northeast Philadelphia as having the finest horses in Torresdale along with neighbor Nelson Brown. Morrell even drove his Tally-Ho carriage from Torresdale to New York in 1887, accepting passengers as he traveled. In 1897, Morrell showed his knowledge of horses as he described his best horse, "the Trotting Bred Stallion which stands 16 hands high, 1150 pounds and has excellent strength and speed." The nearby racetrack on his grounds was used by him personally and for the races run in the summer for the guests of the Morelton Inn. Cookouts and fairs were a common event at San Jose during the summers for friends and children.

In 1893, Morrell became involved in a controversy when Governor Pattison considered him a candidate to head the Third Regiment

Fun and games were always a part of the lifestyle of the rich and famous of Torresdale. Here a crowd from Torresdale gathered around a game, ready to play at the sulky racetrack. *Courtesy of the Archives of the Sisters of the Blessed Sacrament.*

of the Pennsylvania Militia. Objections followed immediately from General George R. Snowden, the commander of the State Militia for Pennsylvania. Snowden claimed that Morrell was a civilian, socially strong and a politician who lacked military discipline. Morrell supporters led by newspaperman George W. Childs replied that it would be a good thing for the National Guard to have a man of Morrell's character leading men. Governor Pattison appointed Edward Morrell a colonel in the state's guard, stating that "the intelligence, ability and business experience of Morrell would bring efficiency to the National Guard." Determined to show his merit for the position, Morrell hired respected military man Philadelphia park commissioner Major Thomas S. Martin to become his tutor. Morrell showed his worthiness for the appointment at his first inspection of the Third Regiment of the militia in Torresdale. It was a memorable sight in July 1893 to see soldiers' tents on the old Knights farm opposite San Michel, with the martial music, booming cannons, prancing steeds and country people gathered around for a week's encampment. On the sixth day of the encampment, Morrell's Third Regiment, the State Fancibles and the Gray Invincibles were out in skirmish drill and using blank cartridges. Each man fired thirty rounds of blank ammunition during the drill, which totaled twenty-five thousand rounds fired during the hour-long practice. Both Colonel Morrell of the Third Regiment and Major Brazier of the Fencibles expressed delight with the conduct and efficiency of the men in their camps. The next morning, the encampment broke up. Tents were taken down, and by noon Knights farm field became its peaceful self.

From the time he met Louise, Edward was committed to her and her causes. He loved her deeply, and in all instances her wish became his command. While his brilliant marriage to Louise had put him in the social register and placed him on the highest rung of the social ladder in Philadelphia, there is little doubt that his first love was Louise. As Louise became more involved with her sister Katharine's work, so too did Edward. He represented Katharine as her lawyer in many property settlements and legal matters. Katharine Drexel was barely one month into her postulancy when Edward Morrell began negotiations for the property on Bristol Pike in Cornwells Heights. He often traveled out west and to the south, visiting schools that

War games and encampments of the Third Pennsylvania Militia under Colonel Edward Morrell took place on the Elizabeth Knights farm in the 1880s and 1890s. The encampments were located directly across Frankford Avenue from the original Drexel summer home San Michel. This home still stands on Frankford/Torresdale Hospital property. *Courtesy of the Archives of the Sisters of the Blessed Sacrament.*

Morrell cattle pens at San Jose, Torresdale, 1890s. *Courtesy of the Archives of the Sisters of the Blessed Sacrament.*

Katharine Drexel had established for African Americans and Indians. By the 1890s, Morrell had become the business supervisor for the St. Francis's Industrial School in Eddington and the Indian Schools, which were built by Mother Katharine Drexel on Indian reservations across America. Morrell continually traveled to these reservations with Louise as a way of supporting Katharine. Morrell was often ill during the last years of his life, but he still carried on the work for Katharine. It was not surprising to find that Colonel Edward Morrell died in Colorado Springs on September 1, 1917, while in transit to an Indian school. The best summary of his life was written the next day by his cousin Mary Powell in a letter to Katharine Drexel: "It was Ned's marriage with that high minded, holy-hearted young girl that has been the full making of his life."

This left Louise Morrell alone in her beloved San Jose, where she spent much of her time traveling with Katharine and then caring for her when she became ill in the latter part of her life. In 1945, Louise passed away, and San Jose became Katharine's property. When Katharine died in March 1955, San Jose became the property of the Archdiocese of Philadelphia and was then sold off piece by piece for housing projects beginning in the 1960s, becoming the Morrell Park area.

***

LIFE OF THE RICH AND FAMOUS IN TORRESDALE

As mentioned previously, Torresdale was the center for wealthy and powerful Philadelphia families in the late nineteenth century and the site of many lavish social events. The mansions along the Delaware River in this area were especially well suited for parties and gatherings. Estates not directly on the river, like those of the Morrell and Drexel families west of Frankford Avenue, did have many social gatherings, but parties were much more audacious and colorful with the sun setting over the sparkling waters of the Delaware. To see guests arrive on their yachts coming across the river from the Rancocas Creek in New Jersey or families like the Biddles and Morrells pull up to the front door in Nelson Brown's famous Tally-Ho coach drawn by four horses was an impressive sight. Adding to the excitement were the

Edward and Louise Morrell's home, San Jose, located four hundred yards west of Frankford Avenue above Grant Avenue. *Courtesy of the Archives of the Sisters of the Blessed Sacrament.*

Walter Garvin with his future wife, Theresa Boyle, both servants in Torresdale. Garvin was chauffeur for the Morrells, while Boyle was second-story maid at the Phillips mansion.

special guests who often attended from other parts of the country or from Europe. World traveler Walter George Smith, who worked with the Vatican and lived near Morelton Inn, could always be counted on to provide foreign visitors to liven up the conversations of the evening. Torresdale in the late 1880s and early 1900s became a center for socialites and was known in Philadelphia as an ideal place for an evening gathering.

What was it like to live in Torresdale in its heyday in the 1880s and 1890s? While the names of the area's wealthy families are well known even today, what was their lifestyle really like? In short, it was a pampered life, lived in elegant settings, with a large domestic staff to attend to every need.

First, to keep a large estate in Torresdale at that time required a corps of domestics that would be unimaginable by most local residents today. At the top of the domestic hierarchy was the butler, who served as a confidant to the woman of the house and was the most important servant of the household. He, in turn, had a parlor maid, a pantry boy and a footman to assist him. Every mansion in Torresdale had a boy usually twelve to sixteen years of age who was often the son of the butler or parlor maid, known as "Buttons." His major responsibility was that of a message boy, an important task in a time when there was no telephone and distances between houses was often great. The Buttons boy dressed in a uniform of his employer's colors with a double row of silver buttons on the jacket of his coat, thus the name. He handed the butler his master's hat, gloves and cane each morning when the master went off to work. Buttons was never entrusted with the master's boutonniere, however, which was always the butler's responsibility. He also received visitor cards on a small silver tray from the guests as they entered for dinner parties. Many times these boys accompanied the head of house to the city on the river steamboat to shop, and afterward they would return with packages to the wife of the house. The boys were very proud of the families for whom they worked, and once in the city with their masters they often staged battles in the streets of Philadelphia to defend the family for whom they worked.

The next person of consequence was the cook, who had complete control over the kitchen, storerooms and contents of the springhouses and icehouses. Working for her were three or four scullery maids who jumped at her command, preparing vegetables, stoking the coal stove,

The Tally-Ho Club of Torresdale was composed of the richest men in Torresdale. Leaders of the club were Nelson Brown, on the left, and Edward Morrell, fourth from the left. *Courtesy of the Archives of the Sisters of the Blessed Sacrament.*

polishing pots or getting supplies from the springhouse. The icehouse contained ice cut from local ponds in the winter and stored in a room lined with sawdust below ground that served as a freezer. The springhouse was a small building located over a running spring in which fresh milk was stored. The milk was placed on shelves near the running spring. The maids carefully ladled off the cream from the milk as it rose to the top of the bottle, so the family could have freshly made ice cream.

Upstairs in the house, the master of the house had his own valet. The mistress also had her own personal maid, and the children had their own governesses and nurses. These large homes with many rooms required several chambermaids to keep the second floor clean and in order. Living quarters for the maid, butler and cook were closed off in the back of the house, entered by a long hall or a back set of stairs.

Outside of the house, three positions were also considered high in status: the head coachman, who had complete control of the stables, horses and carriages; the head gardener, who was responsible for the design of the garden so that there were always blooming, colorful flowers; and the captain of the family yacht, who was responsible for its care and readiness for family use. Estates on the river had a boathouse whose upper part was fitted up as a teahouse, having a fireplace to dispel the dampness from the river below. Refreshments were served here by the butler, usually during the afternoon. Most of these formal estates had a cast-iron deer, fountains or a cast of the family dog looking out over the river. The cast-iron dog at Glen Foerd still "guards" the riverbank today.

To live this life required considerable wealth. In all, we have described the need for some ten domestic workers per family. Such a large domestic workforce raises the question of where all these domestic servants lived. One only has to visit these old estates to realize that there was not enough living space in these mansions to accommodate ten workers. Clearly, there were areas provided in the main house for perhaps two or three servants, but the lower strata of workers had to be housed in a special servant house located a distance from the mansion. For large parties, other workers were hired from a local pool of available people. Still others, like carriage and horse men, lived in the many nearby stables, while yachtsmen could sleep on the yachts anchored in the Delaware River. The area surrounding the original Risdon's Ferry region, Grant Avenue and the river—where in earlier decades local residents had gained employment from the ferry

The Torresdale riverfront mansions were famous for dog statues facing the river. This dog still remains standing at Glen Foerd in Torresdale.

and its commercial activity—was now supported by the social lifestyle that required large numbers of domestic workers and ground crews. No other section in the northeast had such a lifestyle.

In the warm days of the summer months, a buzz of activity usually occurred on the top floor of the boathouse, which was equipped with lounge chairs, a fireplace and a beautiful view of the river. The banks of the river were very high and rocky in the Risdon's Ferry area of the river, so most boathouses had two or three floors with stairs leading to areas on the water below, with a dock nearby to be used by large yachts. Trays of food were set out on open tables from 12:30 p.m. to 3:30 p.m. for lunch. Plans were made for the afternoon, and appropriate staff was provided by the host: carriage drivers and horses for those wishing to ride to the nearby racetrack or a boatman for those who opted for an excursion on the river.

Torresdale's wealthy families maintained their religious practices even though they might only be in the area for the summer months. Most who were Protestant attended All Saints' Episcopal Church on Frankford Avenue near Grant Avenue. A visit to the church's graveyard today and a reading of its tombstones will reveal the many wealthy families of an earlier era buried there. One Protestant family, the Macalesters, built their own Presbyterian church directly across the street from their home on Grant Avenue just east of State Road. The church has since been torn down and a house built in its place. For Catholics like the Drexel, Morrell and Thomas Kilby Smith families, St. Dominic's Church was nearby on Frankford Avenue above the Pennypack Creek. One of the large and magnificently built churches in the region, its tower could be seen from miles away above the farm fields of the day. The wealth of Torresdale's Catholics living in the mansions along the Delaware River can be seen in the grandeur of this church.

This era of life in Northeast Philadelphia has long since passed away and been forgotten. Still, Torresdale was well known in its day and had many famous visitors. Former president Ulysses S. Grant came to Torresdale in the late 1870s and stayed on Grant Avenue in Adolph Borie's home. He reminisced with his former secretary of the navy, Thomas Kilby Smith, in his home on Milnor Street and was an honored guest at a party held for him by the Foerderers at Glen Foerd. All types of guests, including the mayor, senators and city councilmen, came to spend the weekend with one of the Torresdale families. Those were the days when Torresdale was ruled by wealthy families and recognized by everyone in Philadelphia as a special place to be invited for a summer weekend.

***

UPSTAIRS AND DOWNSTAIRS: WORLDS APART

To maintain the previously described lifestyle of the rich and famous in Torresdale required large numbers of servants. It is estimated that Northeast Philadelphia had five hundred servants employed in 1910 in Torresdale. Among them were a few African Americans hired by the Drexel sisters, with the remainder being Irish servants recently arrived in the United States. Much like the conditions depicted in the British television series *Upstairs, Downstairs*, activities in Torresdale were divided into two lifestyles. In our previous stories of the rich and famous, we introduced the lavish lifestyle of the wealthy of Torresdale. Now we will examine the lives of the Irish servants and their struggles to move into the American mainstream.

In Ireland, there were still many issues in the period between 1910 and 1940 that encouraged the move to America. The potato famine was ancient history, but the inheritance laws that followed the English tradition of leaving the oldest offspring the entire estate gave younger children little reason to stay. From 1920 to 1940, there were no Irish immigrant quota laws in the United States, making it easier to come to America. However, immigrants still needed verbal assurance from someone in the United States that work awaited them there. This was not easy in the Depression years of the 1930s. Also, the 1916 Easter Uprising—which was a very nasty shooting war—had caused the government to hunt down Irish Republican Army (IRA) supporters who left the country in droves. Clearly, on the other side of the pond, Irish people were still lining up to come to America throughout these twenty years.

For the women, service in the homes in America was the best way out of Ireland. It was honorable employment that fit their work ethic and religious upbringing. Work as servants provided women with a place to live, three meals a day and a small cash sum that could be put away for a

A group of Torresdale servants gets ready for a trip to the New Jersey shore on their day off. Temporary servant Anna Falls is third from the left.

"rainy day." Irish girls seeking a new life in America had the best chance of avoiding the violence in the streets by being part of the close-knit Irish servant society of Torresdale.

The rules for servants in Torresdale were simple. Loyalty to the family they served was essential. An Irish servant hierarchy in each house formed the network that supervised the employees. Work was judged by a higher-ranking servant based on the completion of assigned tasks. For instance, the cook supervised everyone assigned to the kitchen, and the upstairs maids worked under the maid who served the woman of the house. Servants had a free run of the kitchen and the outdoors at the back of the house but were not permitted in the bedrooms, dining room or parlor when not working. The Irish servants' favorite name for their rich bosses when talking among themselves was "Big Bug," because they remembered in Ireland how the big bugs lived off the little bugs. The one act that resulted in the automatic firing of a servant was stealing. Although there were amicable settlements of issues between servant and master, there were few exceptions to the rule about theft, regardless of years in service or position in the house.

The understanding of how this Irish servant society functioned is based on daily routines in Torresdale. The hardest part of being a servant in

Torresdale was its isolation from Northeast Philadelphia society. Without transportation (except for the Hop, Toad and Frog Trolley line miles away in Holmesburg), there was little for servants to do on days off. Trains were too expensive for them. For this reason, the job with most prestige among servants was the chauffeur position. Walter Garvin, who became driver for Louise Drexel Morrell in 1926, was one of these fortunate individuals. Garvin, who arrived in Bensalem in the early 1920s, became indispensable to the lifestyle of Torresdale servants. Handsome and well liked, with a warm Irish brogue, Walter became the messenger to the outside world, a man who could buy things outside of Torresdale and bring it to the Irish servants.

To know more about Walter Garvin is to know the Irish servant society. Garvin rarely spoke directly to Louise Morrell, despite driving her every day. When he did, he always addressed her as "Madam." Like most in the servant system, he rarely received direct orders from the lady of the house. Garvin received his daily instructions from Leona Colby, longtime secretary to Louise Morrell. As Morrell's companion/secretary, Colby planned her daily schedule and trips to Europe and the western United States. Garvin always referred to her as "Miss Colby" because she was his in-house superior. While they might use nicknames in the kitchen about their rich bosses, the Irish in Torresdale were always respectful when talking to a superior. Garvin was privileged to hear the conversations of the leaders of the Catholic Church in Philadelphia but never repeated a word they said. In his work, Garvin met and formed a friendship with Father James Coakley, founder of the St. Katharine of Siena Church in 1922. Garvin also had a lifelong relationship with the third pastor of the church, Father Thomas Fitzgerald. He was on speaking terms with Cardinal Dennis Dougherty (cardinal 1918–51), the head of the Archdiocese of Philadelphia, who visited Louise Morrell so often that she had a two-bedroom suite built for him at San Jose. Garvin was also close to Mother Katharine Drexel, founder of Sisters of the Blessed Sacrament in Bensalem; she and Louise often rode in the back seat of his limousine on trips. When Walter Garvin married Theresa Boyle, second-floor maid in the Phillips mansion, and left Morrell's service, these experiences gave him confidence when dealing with the public, which eventually made him a leader among the Irish of Northeast Philadelphia.

Similar to the chauffeur position was the laundry truck driver service of Harry McRory, except that his route was confined to the mansions inside

A young Walter Garvin began work at the Morrell mansion as a chauffeur when he arrived in America in the early 1920s.

St. Katharine of Siena Church in Torresdale, the favorite church of the Irish servants of Torresdale.

Torresdale. Nevertheless, he had a car and could move about quickly. Harry McRory was newly arrived from Ireland and idolized Katharine Drexel, whom he served in various capacities for years. They met in the early 1920s when McRory arrived in Torresdale from Ireland. Katharine Drexel had a laundry service established in her Bensalem novitiate to serve the needs of the Sisters of the Blessed Sacrament. When Katharine was asked by the Biddle and Macalester families (big city bankers) requesting to be included in the service, she did so and hired then sixteen-year-old Harry McRory to be the pickup and delivery man for the daily laundry service. The nuns from her order and the children from the Drexel Boarding School for blacks washed and folded the laundry daily. In time, Harry became the unofficial messenger for Torresdale's Irish servants. Events being planned by servants or news from various mansions became part of his conversation for the day.

The most exciting news carried by McRory was the announcement of unauthorized party dates and locations. Organized within the Irish servant communities, these parties were held when many factors came together. Parties and get-togethers were fun for the workers because they

Lizzy Falls, on the right, and Mary Falls in front of the Harrison mansion on a workday dressed in their servant uniforms.

relieved the humdrum existence of servant life. One such party held at the Harrison mansion was triggered by the family leaving on a trip to New York. The night before leaving, a dinner for twenty of Harrison's friends was held. Two obstacles to a servant party had been removed. First, the leftover food from the Harrison dinner would serve to feed the servants at their party; second, the Harrison mansion was to be empty for the weekend. A third happy event occurred when it became clear that no large parties were planned by Torresdale mansion owners for the weekend. McRory announced to all as he traveled that the cook at the Harrison mansion, Mary Falls, had saved the leftover shrimp, tuna and cakes for this very special Saturday night get-together. Word of mouth quickly alerted the Torresdale servants. Despite outnumbering the men five to one, the women loved these parties. Most of the servant couples who were married in Father Thomas Fitzgerald's St. Katharine of Siena Church met at one of these impromptu parties.

Parties were always held in the kitchen, where the food laid out by the cook matched that served to the rich. When Walter Garvin heard the news about the servant party, he automatically knew that his job was to bring Irish whiskey. Also, Irish parties in the kitchens of the Torresdale mansions were never complete without a fiddler. Irish dancing had always been a highlight in Ireland, and it would continue to be so in America. There were many fiddlers available in Tacony, where the largest Irish immigrant population in Northeast Philadelphia lived at the time. Walter stopped by Tacony on one of his trips that week to make arrangements for a fiddler who would play for free, lured by the favorable man-to-women ratio.

Originally, the Catholic church used by the Irish servants of Torresdale was the St. Dominic's Church of Holmesburg. However, it was not popular with them because it was attended by a majority of older German Catholic farmers and reflected old German Catholic values in both type of service and social activities. The Morrell family, knowing the concerns of the Irish servant class about St. Dominic's, helped the Catholic Church purchase the O'Rourke mansion so it could be converted into a Catholic church. The idea was welcomed in Torresdale. Father Fitzgerald, the third pastor, was instrumental in modernizing the building and developing the church.

This was the perfect fit. Fitzgerald was the kind, fatherly type who still had many contacts and friends in Ireland. He was not only the father to the Irish servant but also formed bonds with them that lasted until his death. After all, Fitzgerald's lovable nature and Irish background added to his bonding with the Torresdale flock. Father Fitzgerald himself had immigrant beginnings in Philadelphia. His hard work, spirit and enthusiasm allowed St. Katharine of Siena Church at Grant and Frankford Avenues to become one of the finest churches in Philadelphia.

The relationship between the rich who lived upstairs and the poor Irish servants downstairs was not the same in Torresdale as it was in England. A belief in democracy had caused the rich in America to be more considerate in their treatment of workers. Handling servants in America was usually more humane and accompanied by compromises. The daily personal relationships between the wealthy class and the Irish servants demonstrates the give and take between these two different lifestyles taking place every day in Torresdale. This becomes clear as we recount some of the stories remembered by descendants of these Irish servants.

One story told by Sister Frances Patrice Kirk, a former nun in St. Leo's parish, was about her mother, Elizabeth Falls. Lizzy Falls was the second-story maid for the (money-managing) Harrison family of Torresdale. Her oldest sister, Mary, had arrived in America about 1909 and became the Harrison's cook, eventually rising to the position of running the Harrison mansion. She became responsible for the hiring of new servants, and in that capacity she was able to bring her sisters from Ireland because she could give verbal evidence of work in America. Eventually, three Falls sisters were working full time for the Harrisons, while sixteen-year-old Anna was a temp who also worked part time at Horn & Hardarts Restaurant. The household ran well, despite being made up of the same family, because everyone respected Mary as the boss; to them she was firm but always fair. Mary's power in the household went unquestioned. She selected fresh vegetables each day from local vendors and meat from local farmers to fit her master's desire for certain meals. Good cooks were often thought of as being irreplaceable by rich families. Mary arranged for guests to stay over and was given more authority as things went well. Her family knew of her accomplishments and stood firmly behind her.

A young and energetic Lizzy found it very lonely on days off in Torresdale because everything was so far away and there was little for servants to do. She was working at the Harrisons' with her sisters Mary, Maggie and Anne, recently arrived from Ireland, but even that did not help. One weekend in the 1930s Lizzy and Maggie decided to

Picture of Lizzy Falls and Frank Kirk seated, and Harry McRory and Mary Falls standing, looking out on the Delaware River with the Harrison mansion in the background.

walk to Red Lion Inn on Bristol Pike. There they saw a car dealership that had just opened selling used cars. Curious, they went into the showroom. When Lizzy asked the price of a car, Maggie interrupted, saying, "Servants in Torresdale don't own cars." The salesman told Lizzy that the price of the car was $400, but only $50 down was needed to own the car, adding that if she bought the car, he would teach her to drive on weekends. Lizzy could envision driving the car as she left the showroom. Arriving at the Harrison mansion, Lizzy went directly to her mattress hideaway and counted out $50. She returned to the car dealership the following week and purchased the car, much to the surprise of the salesman, who drove her back to the Harrisons' mansion promising to return in one week to give Lizzy lessons.

Seeing the car, Mrs. Harrison was visibly upset. She was not going to have a car parked in front of her home that detracted from its beauty. Lizzy and Maggie were summoned by Mrs. Harrison to discuss the situation. Mrs. Harrison came right to the point, stating, "Lizzy, you can't have a car." Lizzy and Maggie argued that it was difficult being isolated on off days and that a car would be a great help in adjusting to the isolation. A compromise was reached: the Harrisons found a spot at the edge of their property with a line of trees that hid the car from view. The salesman moved the car to that area and returned over the next three weeks to teach Lizzy to drive. Her favorite trip became a drive to Longshore Street in Tacony to shop or go to the movies. Wonderfully friendly people, St.

Leo's Irish Catholic Church and the many job opportunities in Tacony led many an Irish servant from Torresdale to move there after they left their servant jobs.

As was the case in every Irish community in America, letters were always coming from and going to Ireland. During the Christmas holidays, these letters increased. Walter Garvin received a twenty-dollar gift each year from Louise Morrell, who politely recommended, "Send this money to your mother in Ireland like a good son," which he promptly did. Letters from Walter's sister Bridget in Ireland were simply addressed to "Walter Garvin c/o Louise Morrell, Torresdale, U.S.A."; Louise immediately forwarded them to Walter. Even though the Irish in Torresdale had little money, they always found some to send to their families in Ireland. Many of these letters are now held by the Immigration Center in Ireland because they show the hardship of women like Bridget who were trying to feed and raise ten children during a depression.

Louise Morrell was not Irish but was raised in her youth by an Irish nanny whom she loved dearly. Taught manners and respect for those less fortunate by her nanny, Miss Cassidy, Louise had great feeling and respect for the Irish because of her teachings. Her summer open house Irish tea parties, decorated in green with special Irish four-leaf clovers on the porch of San Jose, were the most anticipated special events for everyone in Torresdale. Louise was loved and honored by the Irish servants as if she were one of them.

It should be noted that these connections with families in Ireland were so strong that when Theresa Boyle, second-floor maid at the Clifford Phillips mansion, was asked in 1936 by Walter Garvin to marry him, she went to her mattress to get money for a return trip to Ireland to ask permission from her family. Returning to Torresdale in 1937, Theresa and Walter Garvin were married in St. Katharine of Siena Church. Walter Garvin then borrowed $600 from his brother-in-law John Boyle and purchased the saloon next to the Northeastern movie house in Wissinoming. His strength of character and Irish friends brought success to his business. He soon had enough to buy a home on Keystone Street in Tacony in St. Leo's parish. Garvin now lived next to his many friends and former servants in Tacony but owned his own home. A get-together of these men usually resulted in a late-night drinking session. Women would stay away from these get-togethers because the conversation usually turned to sending guns to Ireland.

The women were frightened by this but knew that it was a regular part of their conversations. Nevertheless, Tacony offered the servants from Torresdale many opportunities: jobs at Disston, work for their wives in the homes of rich families on Disston Street or work at the Eben-Harding Textile mill. One thing is clear: the Irish succeeded in America because they were hard workers who were able to save money from the most limited salaries.

The Irish atmosphere in Tacony was well known by Torresdale Irish servants. Irish wedding records indicate that most servants who were married by Father Fitzgerald at St. Katharine of Siena Church eventually settled in Tacony. The list included the following families: Sullivan, Kirk, McRory, McDonough, Sheridan and Garvin. The Ancient Order of the Hibernians (AOH) was founded in 1890 in Tacony to support causes in Ireland. This chapter of AOH was the only one in Northeast Philadelphia, although its meetings were attended by Irish from throughout the northeast. Men like Garvin and Kirk joined AOH and promptly became leaders in the organization. Most of the Irish who left servant positions in Torresdale also became members. Walter Garvin, a bartender and bar owner by trade, would only drink milk at these AOH meetings and at his bar because he felt that if he got accustomed to drinking he could easily become an alcoholic. Also well respected in Tacony was Frank Kirk, who was compared in his obituary to the famous Irish martyrs Parnell and Plunkett, who had given their lives for Ireland. Aid to Ireland was an active part of the lives of most Irish in the northeast.

However, the Irish servant society was ending. The number of servants in Torresdale had declined 50 percent by 1940. Originally, the income tax regulation of 1914 gradually took its toll on mansion owners, who had less money to spend. Old money held by individuals was drying up as new money was placed in massive national financial institutions like the Morgans and the Mellons. World War II ended the servant Irish working society of Torresdale when it became impossible for the wealthy—many having lost fortunes in the stock market during the Depression—to hire large servant staffs. They simply could not compete with the salaries offered by factories involved in the war effort. The end of the Irish servant class lifestyle of Torresdale came after World War II.

The story of politics in Northeast Philadelphia during the same period is particularly dynamic. While politics was never discussed between the upstairs rich and the servants, it was becoming an active issue. Mansion owners were all Republicans, many having within their families former

Campaign poster notes Walter Garvin's support for Josh Eilberg.

mayors and congressmen, like former mayors Edwin Fitler and J. Hampton Moore or former congressman Edward Morrell. Downstairs, the new Irish immigrant was turning to Democrats for help.

On the Republican side, Austin Meehan was kingmaker. It seemed as though nothing happened in the northeast without Aus's blessing. On the Democratic side of the fence, it was like the Broadway musical *Fiorello*: Get me "some qualified [Democrat] who's willing to lose," and they always did. In the late 1930s, things began to change as new housing sprung up in the northeast, and many new, younger homeowners registered Democratic. Two obvious leaders of the Democratic Party in Northeast Philadelphia were William J. Green and John F. Byrne. Both were originally from the Fishtown-Kensington neighborhood, and they were good friends. William Green and John Byrne had a "gentleman's agreement" that each would take turns running for Congress from the northeast every two years. In 1942, Green came very close to winning—so close that he abrogated the agreement and challenged Byrne for the Democratic nomination in 1944. With the help of the Irish servant vote, Bill Green won the primary election and then won the general election as a Democratic congressman in Northeast Philadelphia.

The rift between Green and Byrne was smoothed over, and they worked together leading the Democratic Party in the northeast till their deaths in 1965. During that twenty-year span, political operations of the Democratic Party in the northeast were run from John Byrne's establishments, first the bar at 7412 Frankford Avenue and then the Cottage Green at Ashton and Willits Roads. Walter Garvin found it difficult to get into political operations at this time because his bar business location competed with that of John Byrne's. Even harder for Garvin was the fact that he could not leave his tavern to campaign until business hours were over. Despite owning bars that were located nearby, Garvin and Byrne were Democrats and best of friends. When "Josh" Eilberg became the Democratic Party leader after Green and Byrne died, it was then that Walter Garvin became chairman of citizens for Josh Eilberg and active in northeast politics. Garvin helped attract the Irish vote to Jewish candidate Eilberg, and that helped get him elected congressman for Northeast Philadelphia.

Northeast Philadelphia was truly shaped and influenced by the Irish servants of Torresdale. Tacony's English village established by Henry Disston one hundred years before was transformed into a community with large numbers of Irish servants who were free and independent. Tacony became the intermediate step from working as a servant to joining a middle-class neighborhood in America. Northeast Philadelphia was truly part of America's "melting pot."

CHAPTER 3

RAIL AND STEEL ARRIVE IN NORTHEAST PHILADELPHIA

***

George Gandy and the Disston Saw Works

One of the most famous names in Northeast Philadelphia history is Henry Disston, often remembered as the founder of Disston Saw Works and the town of Tacony. Yet, those who have studied him know little about his life or relationship with his family. He is usually pictured as a man of integrity who was loved by the community. Over time, the legend of Henry Disston has outstripped the reality of the man.

The recent discovery in Florida of the diary of George S. Gandy (1851–1946) by researcher R. Dennis Green provides us with the first known record of Henry Disston's family life and personality, as well as a clear description of how the Disston company functioned when it was expanding and moving to Tacony in the 1870s. Through Gandy's writings, we come to see Henry Disston as a real person with all the foibles and character traits of any human being.

Gandy was born in Cape May, New Jersey, on October 20, 1857, the son of a sea captain. He grew to be five feet, two inches tall and came to be called the "runt." Gandy was always defensive about his size and on many occasions fought those who ridiculed him. When he was sixteen, his father went bankrupt, and young George went to Philadelphia, where he studied bookkeeping for three months. At that time, he lived in Northern Liberties near the Disston family home, becoming friends with Henry Disston's sons and having Mary (Henry's only daughter) as a playmate. When he finished bookkeeping school, Gandy went to Disston's Keystone Saw Works as a clerk in the bookkeeping department at four dollars per week. At this time, the Disston factory was located on Front and Laurel Streets in Kensington.

Working in the bookkeeping department, Gandy saw Henry Disston every day. He described Disston as "a rough diamond" who used profanity with the best of men and spoke the common language of the streets. Disston's employees all regarded him as a hard worker who knew the saw business and a man who was very loyal to his friends. Gandy's first run-in with Disston occurred in 1872. It was a year that found Disston stressed over a growing business and a commitment to move the factory to Tacony. During a discussion, he cursed out Gandy in front of the men in the office. The next morning, Disston swore at him again. An annoyed Gandy went to see Disston in his office after work. As Gandy entered the room, Disston never stopping writing, abruptly calling out, "What do you want?" Gandy waited and Disston finally looked up, putting his glasses on the top of his head. Gandy began, "I am only a boy and I don't think I am presuming but I have feelings of a man just the same. I don't like your treatment of me, and I want to quit." A surprised Disston replied, "But George, I didn't mean anything." Gandy liked Disston and accepted his apology. He then offered his boss some advice: "Here is your trouble, you get your mind on something and go with 3 or 4 men to see something and when you come back to the office 5 or 6 people are waiting to see you. Suppose when you get busy you just ring for me."

Henry Disston always liked men who spoke their minds and were loyal, hardworking employees. He had found that trait in longtime family friend George Gandy. In 1872, Disston placed Gandy in charge of the payroll department. On his first day on the job, Gandy informed Disston that he would reorganize the department using his own system. He explained to Disston that the foreman would keep time and pay the men and that he also wanted a timekeeper and for all workers to enter one gate. As they went in, they would be required to hang a brass hook by their number on a board to show that they were being paid to work. The foreman was required to check with the timekeeper and total the hours, submitting them weekly in writing to Gandy. Disston agreed and the new system was put into place.

Gandy's record as controller of the company was outstanding. He recovered over $200,000 in money that had been stolen from the company by corrupt foremen. There were many cases in which men who did not exist were being paid. Disston supported Gandy at every turn. Many of the foremen wanted to continue the old system, in which they presented accounts on a chalkboard that were erased weekly, denying Gandy permanent records of employment. Although many of the foremen had helped create the company and were Henry Disston's longtime friends, he told Gandy, "You handle it, I won't interfere." In addition to rooting out corruption at the factory, Gandy went to customers finding that some Disston saws had been sold with no record of payment to Disston. He showed the record to Disston, who as always left it to Gandy to settle. Gandy found that one supervisor who had worked sixteen years for Disston and was a close friend was the culprit. Gandy got a warrant for his arrest and went to his house. The man admitted to the thefts, and Gandy confiscated his house, a mortgage

Disston, the largest saw company in the world in 1942. George Gandy's foreman profit-sharing plan was one of the reasons for the company's success.

for $3,000 on the house next door, a government bond and $11,300 in cash. During 1872–74, Gandy proved to be the right man for a company that needed controls and a tight financial system. As Henry Disston bought up farmland in Tacony, built houses for his workers and kept the business growing, he was always confident that he had the money available to pay for all of his projects.

After Gandy got the payroll department straightened out, he told Henry Disston to stop constantly enlarging the factory. He challenged Disston, asking him, "What is going to happen if you die? You have 27 foremen, increase their pay. They will make you more money with a business interest and also be increasingly loyal to the factory." Disston did just that. He put the twenty-seven foreman on a profit-sharing contract arrangement. They now had a stake in the profits of the company and became the stabilizing influence in the business for the next seventy years. This arrangement, and Disston's reputation for quality and integrity, became trademarks of the company.

An indication of Henry Disston's respect for George Gandy was made clear when he introduced Gandy to real estate mogul M. Lukens. "Mr. Lukens, this is George Gandy. This is very tough to say. I have 5 boys, but George is more account to me than all of them put together. I'll tell you something you don't know. George is going to marry my Molly [Henry's daughter Mary Disston]. She is my only girl, and I wish she wouldn't get married at all, but rather she would marry George than any man on earth." At the time, Disston was showing his age and according to Gandy would have "periodic drinks at the end of the work day," after which Gandy would take him safely home in the evenings. This drinking habit was a part of Henry Disston's life—this from the man who established Tacony as an alcohol-free town. Gandy's close relationship with Henry Disston created hard feelings between Gandy and the Disston boys, however.

With the approval of Henry Disston, Gandy married Molly Disston in 1876. After two years of marriage, Molly, who suffered from Bright's disease, became pregnant, had a convulsion and had a premature birth that was complicated by her condition; she died in 1878, ten days after her father's death. For George Gandy, life then changed. Three days after Mary's death, three of Henry Disston's sons, led by Hamilton Disston and his attorney, called Gandy into the office. Hamilton stated, "We have always had this business to ourselves and we still intend to keep it that way." Gandy replied, "It is clear you don't want me here anymore, you can get along without me but don't think that I will take your $30,000 offer for my shares of the company." They asked Gandy what would he take, and he replied $50,000. The case went to court, and rumors began to circulate that Gandy had mistreated his wife, had taken advantage of Henry Disston and had little respect for the Disston boys. The real truth was that the brothers had always been jealous of their father's loyalty to George Gandy. On many occasions, requests for money by the boys had been rejected by Gandy, who felt that they were not in the best interest of the company. In the end, Gandy, then a successful owner of many trolley lines in Philadelphia, won his settlement and officially left the company. Final vindication came five years later from Hamilton Disston, who told Gandy over lunch, "George I was a fool to take advice from anyone else. We didn't treat you right. Can you forgive and forget?"

The ironic part of this story is that George Gandy's system, which had placed twenty-seven foremen on a profit-sharing scheme, saved the company during the latter half of the nineteenth century. Hamilton Disston, then president of the company, had little interest in the day-to-day operation of the business. He was a man about town, interested in politics, parties and fishing in Florida. Hamilton became involved in real estate in Florida and would eventually own three-quarters of the state. He was rarely in Philadelphia after 1888, but Disston Saw Works continued to run well because of the structures and systems put in place by Gandy. Hamilton committed suicide in 1896 when his Florida venture went bankrupt, a fact that was kept secret by the family for fifty years, while Gandy went on to build the nation's longest automobile bridge at the time between St. Petersburg and Tampa Bay. Gandy died in Florida in 1946, leaving this record of his early life in Tacony.

***

TACONY'S FOUNDING MOTHER: MARY DISSTON

Not much has been written about Mary Disston (1822–1895), the richest and most influential woman in nineteenth-century Northeast

Philadelphia. While Henry Disston (1819–1878) is generally credited with building Tacony and making it the ideal family-centered, paternalistic industrial town in America, an examination of the events of the time shows that he actually had little to do with the town. His main concern was his saw factory and its move to Tacony from Northern Liberties in 1872. Henry Disston began work on his planned Tacony community in 1876 and put Jonathan Marsden in charge since Marsden had built a home at Keystone and Longshore Streets in 1875 and was living in Tacony. Disston died in 1878, however, only two years after the development of Tacony had begun. Since it took until 1899 to complete the process, these two short years gave Disston little time to influence the character and development of Tacony. Available evidence from those years indicates that the spirit and attitude of the people in the town were nurtured under the gentle hand and guidance of Henry's wife, Mary. The story of how Henry, and not Mary, subsequently received the credit for the development of the utopian community of Tacony tells us much about the neglect by historians of the early contributions of women to American history.

When Henry Disston began planning his move to Tacony, he knew that he would need houses for his workers. Since he and his advisors did not want to mix factory profits with home-building money, he turned to Mary and established the Mary Disston estate. Mary was a strong-willed woman who ran the Disston family and had a tremendous influence on Henry's decisions. Henry placed the purchase of farmland and the building of homes in Tacony under the estate—under Mary's control. This left Henry out of many of the decisions regarding the town and gave Mary much of the responsibility. It was through her benevolence and goodwill that free land was given to schools, churches, firehouses and parks for the benefit of Disston workers. Much of the town's love for the Disston family was due to Mary's ability to understand the community and her willingness to respond to its needs. A devout Presbyterian, she was intensely interested in promoting religious institutions and establishing a more humane social order. Mary was also active in Philadelphia's Social Gospel movement focused on improving conditions with the city's working class.

By the time Henry Disston died in 1878, Mary Disston held mortgages on hundreds of properties in Tacony, Frankford, Bridesburg and Atlantic City. She also owned 20 percent of the Disston Saw Works, which added to her income. In all, Mary Disston's income between 1876 and her death in 1895 averaged $112,000 a year from her estate and close to $60,000 a year from the dividends of the factory, making her the richest and most powerful woman in Northeast Philadelphia. With these funds she pursued Henry Disston's dream of a paternalistic community in Tacony. Churches, schools, playgrounds and home improvements were all paid for by the Mary Disston estate. The town gladly accepted Mary Disston's vision of a child-centered family town. An important factor in shaping Tacony's development were the Disston estate deed restrictions that prohibited the sale of alcohol in the town—a provision still enforced today. Mary's warm nature and belief in helping her fellow man were the building bocks of what became the legend of Henry Disston.

An example of how the Disston family used the estate for the development of the community is found in the building of homes on the 6700 block of Marsden Street. Jonathan Marsden was scheduled to be sent to Sheffield, England, his former hometown, in 1880 to seek skilled steelworkers for the Disston Saw Works. He was to hire the best steelworkers he could find who were willing to relocate to Tacony. Hamilton Disston, Henry and Mary's eldest son, who was then in charge of the company, went to his mother in 1879 to request that the Mary Disston estate build homes for these potential workers from Sheffield. Mary consented and work on the homes began in 1879. Marsden was given plans and sketches of the homes, along with a picture of the elaborate new Tacony Music Hall on Longshore Street to demonstrate the "modern lifestyle of Tacony" to the men he would be recruiting.

The houses to be built on Marsden Street were quite simple in design. A recent visit to the home of Frank and Mary Podorski on the block gives insight into the structure of the dwellings. There were two rooms upstairs and two rooms downstairs, no closets and a first-floor stairway between the rooms. Gas lighting was featured in each room, as was a small gas stove and icebox in the back first-floor kitchen area and an outhouse near a back shed. Water was provided in the house by the Tacony Water Works on Longshore and Cottage Streets (where Disston Playground is today). The street was to be paved with sidewalks and equipped with gaslights, providing all residents

"Battleship Row" on the 6700 block of Marsden Street. Built to house recently hired steelworkers from Sheffield, England, in 1880. This picture was taken in 1900.

with good footing and lighting. The houses had the convenience of a central heating system that consisted of a basement coal furnace, which allowed fumes to go up the chimney and the heat to go to the first floor through a hole in the floor with a grate at the bottom of the first-floor stairs. The second floor was heated by heat going up the stairs. The system was based on heat naturally rising throughout the house. Though not the most efficient system, it was very modern for the time.

This gives us a clue as to the type of worker Hamilton Disston wished to attract from England. First, he wanted young married men just beginning a family who would stay at the factory for many years. Therefore, the homes were built to accommodate no more than two children. When recruiting workers, Marsden emphasized that the rent was only ten dollars per month, which would be only a very small portion of their pay. If workers grew and prospered at Disston Saw Works, there were many larger homes available for them in Tacony. Marsden was able to attract over two hundred young steelworkers to the community, most of whom had wives and small families or were unmarried. Sitting on top of a hill, the twenty-six row homes on Marsden Street looked like a battleship from Torresdale Avenue as the sun set behind them each evening. The new renters soon referred to their houses as "Battleship Row," a name that is used even today. Since all of the new workers were recruited by or worked for Jonathan Marsden in Disston's steel shop, the street was named Marsden Street.

In 1895, when Mary Disston died, "Battleship Row," along with 339 other properties in Tacony, became part of the Mary Disston Estate Trust to be rented to Disston workers only. The trust was to remain active until the last of her grandchildren passed away. The trust was set up to rent homes at a reasonable rate to Disston workers with the income going to Mary's grandchildren. It was Mary Disston's wish at her death that the kind of ruthless industrial capitalism practiced at the time not become part of her estate trust. The trust was not to make excessive money but was first and foremost to benefit the Disston workers and the Tacony community.

By the 1930s, the Mary Disston trust was a highly structured, benevolent and community-centered organization. If local organizations needed money for civic purposes, the trust could always be relied on for a donation. The trust had an office at 4811 Unruh Street, where Catherine Seed was paid to administer the fund. Workers hired at Disston were sent there to rent homes. Catherine collected rents and arranged repairs for 365 homes in Tacony. Included on the list were the "Battleship Row" homes on Marsden Street, as well as homes on Wissinoming Street called the "Mary Seven" that had been rented to African Americans since 1919. In 1939, Catherine Seed reported that rents ranged between eighteen and twenty-five dollars per month. For those who missed paying rent, their names were put on "The List" and given to shop foreman Burt Castor, who then withheld the overdue rent from the following week's pay. If a worker continued to be late with the rent, Castor would deduct it from his pay automatically.

After the death of Mary Disston's last grandchild in 1942, the estate trust was liquidated as per Mary's will. By 1944, all of the Mary Disston Estate Trust homes had been sold. The trust adhered to Mary's request that the houses be offered to the lessee first and that they be put into good repair, including roof, plumbing and even new wallpaper. The prices of the homes were set at $2,500 for those on Van Dyke Street, $2,700 for Hegerman Street and $1,875 for "Battleship Row" on Marsden Street. The homes were quickly purchased by renters exercising their option to buy as mandated by the trust. Catherine Seed forwarded the proceeds from the sales to the Disston family to be divided equally among them. She also proudly reported to them that only one home had been sold to the general public. All of these benefits to Disston workers greatly enhanced the Disston family's reputation in Tacony, but most of the credit went to Henry Disston. It is clear that the people of Tacony had a hard job separating good things done in the community by the Mary Disston Estate Trust from the Disston Saw Company.

Although she has been generally neglected by historians, Mary Disston did more to make Tacony the famous, paternalistic, family-centered town than did her husband. It was her gentle, guiding hand that nurtured the respect and love of Tacony's residents toward the Disston family. Mary Disston, like many of the women of her day, ended up as a footnote in the history of her famous husband rather than the real heroine of the Tacony story. Thankfully, today we can correct this misconception and give her the credit she deserves.

***

Workers Unite Wissinoming

The history of Wissinoming as a residential community begins in 1885 in Fishtown when a group of textile workers in local factories were discussing a healthier place for their children to grow up. Many of the men were supervisors or machinery repair men who were earning good money at the time. Employees of the Martin Laudenberger Hosiery Mill at 1101–1103 Frankford Avenue were leaders in the discussions. The Fishtown area at the time was overcrowded with homes on narrow streets, and the air was often filled with the smoke from the numerous factories in the area. A solution suggested by one of the men was to move to the northeast section of the city where there was open land and fresh air. A section that had been skipped

A picture taken in 1909 of the Wissinoming Improvement Association: President John J.L. Merget, third row extreme right, William J. Duryea, second from left top row, and Reverend Charles J. Faunce, second from left bottom row. This is the group that led Wissinoming during its early years.

over for development when Henry Disston founded Tacony in 1872 was still available. A committee was formed by the Fishtown group to investigate this cooperative idea of building and purchasing homes.

The committee found that a two-hundred-acre section of land then known as the Howell farm (Howell Street is named after the old farm) was for sale and could be purchased for the right price. The land was located between where Torresdale Avenue is today (Torresdale Avenue was then called Emiline Street) and the Robert Cornelius estate, which is now Wissinoming Park. The committee raised the money for the purchase of the Howell farm from one hundred Fishtown textile workers and formed itself into the Wissinoming Land Company. This allowed the group to purchase the two hundred acres and break it into small building lots. These lots were then sold to the members at a reasonable price so they could start building homes. The Wissinoming Land Company eventually led to the formation of the Wissinoming Improvement Association to run the town. This was the first such association in Northeast Philadelphia.

Prominent in this early development of Wissinoming were President John J.L. Merget, William J. Duryea and Reverend Charles J. Faunce, all leaders of the Wissinoming Improvement Association. It was clear from the beginning that the association had as its goal the establishment of a residential community with little or no industry in the town. The only industry developed within the community was Edwin H. Fitler's Cordage Works at 5625 Tacony Street, two miles southeast of the new residential living area. By 1891, the American Cordage Manufacturers Association recognized Fitler's company as one of the largest producers of rope in the United States. Fitler's factory was important to Wissinoming since many of the former textile workers quit their jobs in Fishtown to work at Fitler's and be closer to their new homes. Edwin Fitler, who lived in Torresdale near the Glen Foerd estate, was important to the region for another reason: he served as mayor of Philadelphia from 1887 to 1891, one of the few mayors who came from Northeast Philadelphia (the other two were William Green and J. Hampton Moore). As mayor, Fitler helped the northeast by advocating for a trolley route to connect Wissinoming and Tacony to downtown Philadelphia.

Early Wissinoming consisted of large farms and two beautiful estates: the Robert Cornelius estate on Bristol Pike (now Frankford Avenue) and Comly Street, and the Matthias Baldwin estate west of State Road and Benner Street. When Cornelius died in 1893, his estate was sold to William J. Kerns, who purchased portions of the land from Cornelius's son-in-law George Bodine. Between 1890 and 1900, the German-Turners Cycle Club rented a building from Bodine and developed a flourishing business renting bicycles for weekend excursions north on Frankford Avenue. A ride to Holmesburg and back was a popular biking activity at the time—bicycles were the fad of the day and Northeast Philadelphia was central to the action. Eventually, the City of Philadelphia purchased Cornelius's land and established Wissinoming Park on the site. This was prompted in part by the desire to preserve the many trees from around the world that Cornelius had collected and planted on the property.

The Matthias Baldwin mansion was located on the opposite side of the new village of Wissinoming. It was built in 1859 by Matthias Baldwin, who began his career as a watchmaker on the corner of Frankford Avenue and Orthodox Streets in Frankford. He went on

The Baldwin mansion, which later became "the Old Ladies Home," in the 1920s on State Road. Baldwin had the railroad station built directly across the street from his mansion for his convenience.

to become the owner of the Baldwin Locomotive Works at Broad and Spring Garden Street and one of Philadelphia's wealthiest men. To stay close to his Frankford roots and his church, St. Mark's of Frankford, he chose to build his summer estate in Wissinoming on the Delaware River. He also used his influence to build a train station located directly across the street from his mansion. This would become Wissinoming Station on the New York to Philadelphia line. Upon his death, the Baldwin mansion was sold in 1888 to the Mapother sisters. They had previously owned an old folks' home in Harrowgate called Mapother Hall and another home at Frankford Avenue and Clearfield Street. Seeking larger quarters for their developing enterprise, they purchased the beautiful Baldwin estate, which offered a beautiful view of the Delaware River. Unlike the 1872 Forrest Home for Aged Actors in Holmesburg, which housed about a dozen residents, this was a massive undertaking for the time. It became known as the Old Ladies Home and housed between 130 and 150 women. Considered one of Philadelphia's largest welfare institutions, admission was granted to those who paid an entrance fee to cover room and board during the life of their stay. The house was an important source of jobs as cooks and housekeepers for local residents.

Within the community of Wissinoming, the advocacy of the Improvement Association promoted other developments. One of the first came in 1888 when Wissinoming Fire Company, now Engine 52, was established and a town hall was opened for meetings. Yet another important project for the association was its efforts to cooperate with Tacony to promote the continuation of Torresdale Avenue to Erie Avenue and add a trolley line on the route, thus completing direct transportation to center city. Most active in the project were contractor Walter Costello and realtor Frank J. Clarke, who had the work completed in 1903. With this important transportation link established, the building of homes in Wissinoming escalated, and the community became a bustling little town with grocery shops, stores, a bank and a movie house, the Elite. Dubbed the "Holy City," Wissinoming became home to nine churches, almost twice the number found in the larger community of Tacony. The Lawton School opened on Benner Street in 1902, and a few years later the Wissinoming Yacht Club opened. It numbered 119 members and fifty-four boats and held annual regattas for the community over the next thirty years.

The most recognized Wissinoming personality in 1900 was Casper Knobel. Few remember him today, but at the time his name was part of the historic folklore of Northeast Philadelphia. It was claimed that during his service in the Civil War Knobel was responsible for the capture of Confederate president Jefferson Davis in 1865. As the story went, he was in the advanced guard of Union forces chasing Davis through the state of Mississippi, eventually finding him and arresting him on behalf of the United States government. Whether the story is true is unverifiable, but few doubted it in Wissinoming.

Given the motives for its founding, it is not surprising that there were only two large companies established in Wissinoming. We have already discussed the Fitler Cordage Works, which has long since closed. The other company was Louderback Moving and Storage Company, founded in the 1940s on the 5900 block of Torresdale Avenue. Originally a local family-owned firm, it grew into one of America's largest and most successful moving and storage firms during the 1970s. It was the forerunner of Louderback North American Vans of King of Prussia, still a nationally known firm today.

One of the important aspects of Wissinoming's early history is that it established an early pattern of land development that would be followed later in other northeast communities. The process of filling in unused parcels of land left unsettled between older, established communities became the pattern of development in Northeast Philadelphia throughout the twentieth century. These sections of land were often small, named by or after the builder. Row homes were popular at first, but many twin and single homes were built later. Crescentville and Lawndale followed Wissinoming in the 1920s, Mayfair in the 1930s, Rhawnhurst in the 1950s and Morrell Park in the 1960s—all are examples of this trend.

***

FRANKFORD: THE HUB OF THE AFRICAN AMERICAN COMMUNITY

The African American population in nineteenth-century Philadelphia was greatly affected by overall population trends in the city. An examination of the 1820 census indicates that 20 percent of the population in Philadelphia was black. African Americans were an important part of the city's economy, working as servants in the houses of wealthy whites, as dockworkers unloading ships in what was then a port city and at other labor jobs. Northeast Philadelphia had a similar pattern of blacks working in the households of the wealthy landowners or working in the gristmills and quarries along the Pennypack Creek. According to the 1890 census, however, only 3 percent of Philadelphia's population was African American. While the actual black population had tripled since 1820, the city had been overwhelmed by immigrants from Ireland and Germany, causing the percentage of blacks to whites to decrease. In the period between 1890 and 1920, a new wave of immigrants from Russia, Italy and Poland would decrease the percentage even further. Racial discrimination and fewer work opportunities for blacks gave rise to pockets of African Americans in enclaves—self-contained communities that increasingly relied on themselves for goods and services. While these changes

Frankford's black population in the 1920s was interested in children and family life. Here a black family babysitter also has a white child among the children she watched.

resulted in fewer jobs for African Americans in the central part of Philadelphia, they did not have the same effect in the more sparsely populated areas of the northeast.

A newspaper article written in the late twentieth century by African American Elwood Budd on file at the Historical Society of Frankford describes how this population shift affected Northeast Philadelphia blacks. Budd describes how Frankford blacks developed within their community the resources to provide for the health and vital services needed to flourish. While the surrounding white population knew little about life in these communities, African Americans were continually updating themselves as to available opportunities and services at various social gatherings.

By the 1930s the changing landscape of the northeast had resulted in three main enclaves of blacks clustered outside of Frankford. These were in Holmesburg, Tacony and in the area on Ashton Road above Holme Circle. The small cluster of blacks living in Byberry in the nineteenth century had dissipated when black abolitionist Robert Purvis moved back to center city Philadelphia after the Civil War. The three remaining enclaves were held together by the African Americans of Frankford, which became the center for connecting all blacks in Northeast Philadelphia.

When there was an illness in the family, Frankford had three black doctors—Dr. Walter Levy, Dr. R.R. Tolver and Dr. Edgar Clark—who were ready to respond to the health needs of African Americans in Northeast Philadelphia. Also, there was an African American dentist, Dr. Edmond J. Presley, at 1512 Overington Street, who served the black communities of Frankford, Holmesburg and Tacony. Dr. Presley practiced dentistry in Frankford for over twenty-five years and became one of the most prominent African Americans in Northeast Philadelphia. He was also known across the city as a member of the Philadelphia Periodontal Society, a member of the American Red Cross Board and a vice-chairman of the welfare group Red Feather. In 1953, Presley was editor of the souvenir program book for the National Dental Society Convention held in Philadelphia. There was also an African American pharmacy in Frankford owned by Dr. Richard Cooper. He shared the business with Philadelphia's only black female pharmacist, Lillian Whitfield.

Black family life in Northeast Philadelphia was very much like that of their white counterparts. Pictured here is an unknown black family living in Frankford.

Food needs were met by neighborhood grocer "Duke" Pittman at Orthodox and Mulberry Streets. For home repairs there were three paperhangers, Edward Flemmins, Edward Shirley and Mozzel Michael. A black contractor, "Ben" Tucker, was available to take care of roofing and cementing needs. In addition, there was an African American horse stable run by Richard "Chick" Craig and his son, jockey Richard "Junior" Craig, that rented horses to blacks in the northeast so that they, too, could enjoy rides in Pennypack Park. Frankford had three barbershops owned by Mr. Jenkins, John Shotwell and Theodore "Barnzie" Barnes. For black children there was even a candy store with special treats at Tackawanna and Herbert Streets, run by Mr. and Mrs. Roman Black. Religious needs were met with three different churches, Campbell AME Church, Second Baptist and the St. Thomas United Methodist. While there were separate black elementary schools, for high school blacks in Northeast Philadelphia could attend Wilson Jr. High, Harding Jr. High and Frankford High along with whites. Frankford's close-knit black community had its own structure, supported by a skilled workforce that would allow it to survive the Great Depression of the 1930s.

Prominent among civic leaders of the Frankford African American community was Samuel W. Smith. His moving and trucking business at 1728 Meadow Street, still owned and operated today, gave employment to many young blacks of the community. Smith's family had lived in Frankford from the early part of the nineteenth century. Besides his lucrative business, Smith found time to be a leader in his church and in community activities. He attempted to organize an African American chamber of commerce in the 1950s, believing that black leaders in the Frankford community should merge their interests with those of the whole northeast for the benefit of all. Never successful, Smith's idea does show the concern that Frankford blacks had for other African Americans in the northeast.

Frankford resident Harry Lowber, a retired railroad employee and a resident of the Frankford community for fifty years, further illustrates the interconnection of the northeast African American community. Lowber lived at 1618 Kinsey Street, having bought the house in 1911. A member of Campbell AME Church, he raised his family there. By the 1950s, his son was working at the post office and living in Tacony, and a second son was living in Holmesburg. This movement between the African American enclaves demonstrates the closeness of these black communities.

The history of the Frankford African American community in the early to mid-twentieth century demonstrates the professional achievements and organization of the black community that had developed in Northeast Philadelphia. Although largely unnoticed by the larger white population, the services provided by Frankford blacks allowed the development of close connections among blacks throughout the northeast.

CHAPTER 4

NORTHEAST PHILADELPHIA TAKES ON A NEW CENTURY

***

TACONY: TWO WORLD WARS AND A DEPRESSION

The recruitment patterns established in the Civil War—where whole towns enlisted into the same regiment—led directly to how Tacony men entered World War I. Dr. Elmer E. Keiser, a graduate of the University of Pennsylvania Medical School, had established his practice in Tacony in 1906 after being appointed Holmesburg Prison doctor. He was so popular in Tacony that he was able to recruit the men of the town to join Company M, First Regiment of the State Militia. He trained the men one night per week as ambulance drivers and in first aid. This was very popular at the time since men got a chance to learn how to drive and also learned first aid at the same time. The community liked the training and most families embraced it. However, it also meant that men in one large block could be called off to war at any time. This happened in 1916, when the men were sent to aid troops from Pennsylvania then engaged in a Mexican border dispute in Texas. When World War I broke out, the unit already in the army was sent to Camp Hancock in Augusta, Georgia, to be reorganized for war in France as the 110th Field Hospital Regiment.

Tacony Ambulance Corps members leave Tacony for Texas in 1916. Families assemble at Tacony Station to see them off.

Having all their boys in one unit kept the community informed about daily happenings in their lives. No sooner had the troops reached Georgia than Edmond Roberts, secretary of Disston Saw Works, learned that the Tacony boys did not have saws to cut firewood. They were cold at night, lacking sufficient wood for fires. He rushed an order of saws free of charge to his "community away from home." Paul Biemuller, son of the local Lutheran minister and a former Disston employee, reported that the saws were "distributed amongst the 'Disston Boys' immediately upon receipt…They all had to try them right away; so glad that at last they had a decent saw to cut firewood. It sure was a pleasure to use the best saw on the market."

Nevertheless, there was great concern at the Disston Saw Works. The war had increased government contracts and brought massive orders for light armor for tanks and shields for navy guns. The Henry Disston Company had been prepared for its workers to stay weeks in Mexico but soon found that the company could not complete the new government war contracts without these men. For the first time, Italians were hired en masse at the factory, and supervisors Harry and Edmund Whittaker were sent by train to Remington, Virginia, to hire black workers. Two hundred workers arrived one week later in Tacony in boxcars and were immediately given jobs by Disston. The boxcars doubled as living quarters for the new workers. The ethnic pattern and racial makeup of the town changed because of the war.

When the Tacony Ambulance Corps was to go overseas to France, one of the men phoned to alert the town that the train taking them to New York from Georgia would travel through Tacony Station. Engineer John Costigan, a resident of Tacony, arranged his schedule to be conductor of the train out of Washington. He stopped the train at Tacony Station despite orders to the contrary from the military. Costigan wired his superiors that the train was stopped because of a "hot box" that required three hours to repair. The whole town alerted, men, women and children in nightclothes headed for the station at 3:00 a.m. for a last goodbye to their loved ones. Privately, Costigan admitted, "I couldn't come back to Tacony and face the people if I went through to New York knowing I had the boys from Tacony on the train. Further, my mother would disown me. I would never think about not stopping the train." Throughout the war, Tacony proved to be a very patriotic community. Letters from Tacony boys were printed locally in the *Tacony New Age* and the *Disston*

The official opening of the Armor Plate Factory built by the federal government for Disston Saw before World War II began in 1940.

Bits. Mothers gathered at Disston Playground once a month to read letters from their sons to one another. Since the boys served together, letters about conditions in France were relevant.

The community received exciting news on August 17, 1918, when the *Public Ledger* reported that two Tacony boys were the heroes of the encounter at the front in France. On August 9 and 10, Mike Biemuller, son of Tacony's Lutheran minister, and Albert Baker evacuated twenty-eight men from the battlefield in Fismette, France. Ten of the thirteen ambulances of their company had been destroyed by shellfire. Under fire and with disregard for their own personal safety, they evacuated men and ambulances. With just three ambulances, they labored forty-eight hours, driving through a shell-swept and gas-infested area to evacuate all wounded soldiers.

Soon after the notice appeared in the *Public Ledger,* crowds with American flags and banners formed outside the two soldiers' residences. Mrs. Anna Baker of 3027 Longshore Street greeted her friends in front of her house, telling them, "It's just great. I'm an American and I feel just so proud of that boy of mine." The Reverend Andreas Biemuller at 6812 Jackson Street shouted the news to his wife as he greeted the crowd outside his house. Biemuller, with justifiable pride, let everyone known how his son had driven the ambulance that had saved so many soldiers' lives in France. Later, when Mike received the Distinguished Service Cross from General Pershing, the whole town attended special services held by Reverend Biemuller.

Impromptu parades occurred throughout the war. The largest of these parades took place on July 22, 1918, when William Disston led the workers from the factory at noon in a spontaneous outburst of loyalty and support for the boys in Europe. Marching up Longshore Street to Torresdale Avenue and then back down Disston Street to the factory, the workers were greeted by families waving American flags. Even individual blocks had celebrations; a "Liberty Sing" was organized by residents of Van Dyke Street between Unruh and Magee Streets, a block that had seven boys in the war.

World War I left Tacony in a good mode; only two men from the ambulance corps had lost their lives, with another sixteen killed when they enlisted in regular fighting units. Things quickly returned to normal as black workers at Disston were let go and the Italians were again relegated to the end of the line when applying for jobs at Disston Saw.

However, the effects of the 1929 stock market crash changed the happiness to dismay. The decline in construction work reduced the market for lumber and thus for tools. When carpenters faced 50 percent unemployment and hardware stores closed by the dozens, Disston was bound to suffer. These circumstances led to a drop in the workforce from 2,500 in 1925 to 1,400 in 1933.

Layoff patterns during the Depression also encouraged unionization. At Disston, unskilled middle-aged workers were likely to lose their jobs to younger workers who were paid a starter salary. Every effort was made to keep skilled workers because they were too difficult to replace. Skilled workers were offered the opportunity to share the available work orders so that they continued to get paid, but a lesser amount. Saw smither William Rowen remembered those days well. He lacked carfare or money for anything extra around the house. His entertainment on Saturday night was to walk to Frankford Avenue and Rawle Street, looking in store windows with his wife, and then return home. The new Liberty movie house on Torresdale Avenue in Tacony remained half empty since some people of the town could not afford the ten-cent admission fee.

During these difficult years in Tacony, the benevolence of the company was apparent to the town of Tacony. Disston would advance wages so workers could pay their bills, no Disston mortgage owned by the Mary Disston estate was foreclosed and late rents were always acceptable without penalty. At Darriff's grocery store, a long list of residents who owed money was kept next to the cash register. Deliveries continued to be made to families, who paid when they could. Darriff remembers the one exception was a woman who owned the boardinghouse at Disston Street and Keystone Street—she never paid off her $2,000 debt.

The coming of World War II ended the depression in Tacony. In 1939, the air force realized from the air battle over Britain that light armor plate was needed in fighter planes to protect the pilot. The only company capable of producing such hard, light steel was Disston. So the government paid for a new steel armor plate building in early 1940 to make seat backs for fighter planes. The war had not yet begun, and Disston was in need of one thousand men for the new plant. This led to the building of low-cost defense workers' housing in Holmesburg at what is now Pennypack Woods and on Roosevelt Boulevard in Northeast Village located where the Internal Revenue Service (IRS)

Tacony had many wartime heroes visit the town during World War II. Lieutenant Thomas Griffin, a pilot under General Doolittle's command during the 1942 raid on Tokyo, visits Tacony in July 1942 and receives a Disston saw from worker Elizabeth Christensen of Tacony.

building stands today. All of these changes occurred prior to the war and led the northeast out of the depression much earlier than the rest of the city.

Once the war began, signs were everywhere that there was plenty of work. The Holmesburg Poor House, normally full, stood empty. All

John Garfield and a fellow actor stand on the porch at 6508 Tulip Street, getting ready to shoot the movie *Pride of the Marines* in 1942.

A Hollywood production crew spent weeks in Tacony preparing for and shooting the movie. It was considered at the time to be the greatest excitement that Tacony had ever seen. Here the crew gets ready for shooting a scene at Schmid's house on Tulip Street in 1942.

construction had stopped. Mayfair and Holmesburg were littered with houses half finished or lots that were prepared for construction left empty. All available labor was needed to man the U.S. war machine centered at the Frankford Arsenal, Disston Saw, Dodge Steel and Cramp Shipyard.

Houses displayed the serviceman star in windows to let passersby know that they had someone in the service. Antiaircraft guns were placed in Tacony Park, with a platoon of soldiers operating them to protect the Tacony-Palmyra Bridge from attack. All nearby airports were closed, with trucks blocking the runways to guard against a surprise attack. Victory gardens were everywhere, and no one discarded fat or rubber tires—they were recycled for the "Boys Over There."

The most notable war event for Northeast Philadelphia was the story of one of America's greatest World War II heroes, Al Schmid. On August 21, 1942, during the Guadalcanal campaign in the Solomon Islands, Schmid's single-handed action held off four hundred Japanese in the Battle of the Tenaru. Schmid was awarded the Navy Cross "for heroism in the line of duty as a machine gunner. Schmid's machine gun squad was attacked by the enemy. Lacking protection from rifle men, it was necessary to tear down their frontal protection in order to meet the charge of the Japanese." In the ensuing fight, all in his squad were wounded, and Schmid was found by the relief squad still holding his machine gun with more than two hundred dead Japanese on the battleground in front of his position. Blinded by a mortar shell, Schmid had spent the night shooting at sounds. He immediately became a national hero, and the movie *Pride of the Marines*, starring John Garfield and Eleanor Parker, both big time Hollywood stars, reenacted his life. During the making of the movie, it was a daily treat for Taconites to seek out Garfield, Parker and the movie crew from Hollywood as they shot scenes for the movie at Schmid's home at 6508 Tulip Street. Tacony seemed at the time to be the center of the world.

All of Philadelphia turned out to welcome Schmid when he returned home in 1942. Walter Annenberg of the *Philadelphia Inquirer* handed Schmid a Hero's Award and a $1,000 check at a citywide celebration at Rayburn Plaza. The speaker, Judge Vincent A. Carroll, encouraged the blind hero, saying, "The light of your eyes has not dimmed because you have taught Americans to see the means to ultimate victory through sacrifice." As in World War I, Tacony had its hero—but this time one who would be shared with the nation.

***

AMERICA'S FIRST GYMNASIUM

Northeast Philadelphia is filled with sports-loving fans who are among the most rabid in the country. Many of them attend games at local gyms to participate in basketball leagues. When questioned, most don't have any idea where the first gym in the United States was located or how gyms became part of the American way of life. Most northeast residents will be surprised to learn that the first gymnasium ever built in America was in Frankford.

To understand how gymnasiums came into being, we must go back to the 1870s following the Civil War. Dr. Charles Evans, attending physician at the Frankford Friends Hospital on Roosevelt Boulevard, was attempting to change the treatment provided for mentally ill patients at the hospital. He recommended a shift away from the ideas of bloodletting and drug use to a program that would increase reliance on more diversified treatments. What was needed in his opinion was increased exercise, baths and electric shock treatment along with a regimen of rest and occupational therapy. From its inception, exercise had always been a part of patient treatment at Friends Hospital, but it was limited to walking the grounds, men working on the hospital farm growing food or women doing household chores. As work therapy gave way to recreational therapy, mid-nineteenth-century treatment became more fun. Patients were encouraged to play tennis or cricket or ride the circular railway constructed for patients on the hospital grounds. A special "swing for exercise" invented by Joel H. Ross of New York City in 1845 was the first exercise device brought on to the grounds of the hospital in the 1870s. This led to the use of organized gymnastics classes with dumbbells in the 1880s, which were brought indoors using hallways and every available space. In 1887, the hospital received a large donation of money for patient care. Knowing the success that the gymnastic program was having with patients, the board of managers decided to build a house that would feature gymnastics and exercise. So it was that the Friends

Hospital opened a specially constructed building that was called a "gymnasium" in 1889.

The gymnasium, the first of its kind in America, was erected on the west front lawn of the hospital and dedicated exclusively to physical activity and physical skills for the patients. The building was to be specially built with high ceilings, ropes to climb, dumbbells, mats and rings. Since bathing and cleanliness were an important part of the exercise treatment, showers were provided for patients to use after exercise. There were no basketball baskets or lines on the floor since no games were played in the gym. The 1890 picture of the exterior of the building shows the large number of patients using the facility at the time. Unfortunately, the gym was built on the Friends Hospital front lawn west of the main building. When Roosevelt Boulevard was widened and extended to Oxford Circle in 1914, the gymnasium was demolished after only twenty-five years of use.

The trend toward physical exercise as a cure for mental illness mirrored events taking place in the real world outside of institutions. First to recognize the importance of a gymnasium was the United States Army at West Point. In 1890, Colonel Herman J. Koehler was appointed the first physical trainer at West Point. He opened the gym at West Point in 1892, three years after the Frankford Friends gym. Koehler ordered the following equipment for his program: one horizontal bar, two horses, one swing, parallel bars, dumbbells and ropes suspended from the ceiling. By 1905, he had enlarged the army gym to include tennis and fencing.

The idea for the equipment to be used in gyms came from yet another movement. The German immigrant population brought to America Frederick Ludwig Jahn's ideas of a "sound body and a sound mind" developed in Germany in the nineteenth century. The ideas had long been a part of German culture, where things like the horse, parallel bars, rings and ropes imitated the physical skills used in life. Jahn initiated these ideas in 1811 when his native Germany was oppressed by Napoleon. Beginning in 1910, German immigrants began forming Turner Gymnasiums across America featuring some of the same gymnastic equipment found at Frankford Friends Hospital and West Point. One of the largest of these gyms was Turner Hall, opened in 1910 at Broad Street and Columbia Avenue in Philadelphia.

The American gymnasium would have gone unchanged if it were not for a Canadian, Dr. James Naismith. He left McGill University to take

A picture of the outside of the first building in America constructed specifically as a gymnasium. Notice patients waiting to use the gym. The building was torn down in 1911 to allow Roosevelt Boulevard to go through.

The only picture of the Friend's Hospital gym from the inside. Note the high ceilings, ropes, mats, rings and dumbbells in place ready for use.

a position at a YMCA in Massachusetts. Naismith was frustrated by the cold New England winters that prevented physical programs in the winter months. In 1891, using a peach basket, he developed a concept for a new game. He wanted a game that would emphasize skill and not strength, as was the case in gymnastics. Ironically, Naismith felt that this would give everyone an equal chance when playing. It was this emphasis on putting a ball into a basket that gave the game immediate popularity. Naismith wrote only thirteen rules for the game, calling it basketball. It was a great success because all you needed was a room with a peach basket at either end and a ball (soccer-type balls were used at first). From 1893 to 1903, the players in the game had to take the ball out of the peach basket after each score. The first college game was played in 1896 between the University of Iowa and University of Chicago, won by Chicago 15–12. The slow movement of the game frustrated the players. It was not until 1903 that Naismith placed a net under the rim to modernize the game.

At the time, there were no gyms in any of the schools of the northeast. The original Jacobs, Crispin, Henry Disston, Lower Dublin Academy and J.H. Brown Schools were all built prior to the concept of a "gymnasium." All physical activity was done outside the building. The first local community advocating a gym in school was Holmesburg. It was not until after World War I that they petitioned the school district for lights for a third-floor attic space so that it could be used for playing basketball at night. Turned down by the school district, the community allowed a local group of men to install the wiring for the lights. At that point, baskets were affixed to either end

The J.H. Brown School in Holmesburg organized a basketball team soon after completion of work on the third-floor recreation room in 1920. The first coach was a woman.

of the room, and the school had its first basketball team in the 1920s, coached by a female teacher.

This became a national trend as schools converted open space into basketball courts. It was not unusual to have a court with pillars in the center of the floor or corners of the court that featured staircases. Walls were often sidelines, and there was no uniformity for these makeshift early gyms. Frankford High School, built in 1913, had two recreational rooms built into the school, one of which had a full basketball court. After World War I, newly built schools, if they were to be considered modern, all had to feature a gymnasium for basketball use. The American gymnasium had moved away from gymnastics to large adaptable spaces that could be used for basketball and other games.

It is clear from this story that the first gymnasium in the United States was built in Northeast Philadelphia and had little to do with sports. Nevertheless, the modern-day concept of what a gymnasium is had its roots in institutions for the mentally ill and not sports institutions.

***

SUNDAY DRIVES ON ROOSEVELT BOULEVARD

When the automobile first came on the scene, it was considered to be for recreational use on weekends. Sunday was a favorite time for a trip to the country or a swim area for relaxation and fun. Cars remained parked for weeks at a time as men continued to take trolleys and trains to work. Roads in the northeast were poor and in some places impassable, having been originally constructed for horse and carriage. However, the opening of Roosevelt Boulevard with its natural beauty and tree-lined streets provided northeast residents with the ideal Sunday recreational activity. A trip to the city limits on the boulevard to see a bear chained at a gas station in Bucks County or a visit to the many airports in Bustleton became the popular thing to do.

Few, if any, of the thousands of people who drive Roosevelt Boulevard every day know the history of this major city thoroughfare. Roosevelt Boulevard got its start in 1902 when Philadelphia mayor Samuel H. Ashbridge proposed what he called the Torresdale Boulevard. His plan

Cars being sold in Bustleton in the 1920s at a Chevrolet/Studebaker dealership. Is it any wonder that the inadequate streets of the northeast became cluttered with cars?

was to build a twelve-lane French-style boulevard that could be used by families who wished to take scenic automobile rides into the countryside. This became a popular activity in the 1920s when the reasonable sale price of the Model T Ford allowed the middle class the opportunity to become car owners.

What became Roosevelt Boulevard started as a three-hundred-foot right of way from Broad Street and Hunting Park Avenue and then followed old roads as much as possible to Torresdale. At the time, the area was largely a farming community traversed by dirt roads—roads that connected the towns of Frankford, Tacony, Holmesburg and Bustleton. The new boulevard, as it was built, was meant to stay as near as possible to these towns without actually entering them. Those advocating the project, many of them northeast residents, saw the boulevard as a direct connection to city hall. In a time when automobiles were coming into widespread use, most were predicting the necessity of a road to link the city and the northeast.

The boulevard was built in sections from Broad Street north, with the sections being opened as they were completed. The first section was opened to Hunting Park in 1903 and then one to Fifth Street in 1907, Oxford Circle in 1911 and finally Pennypack Circle in 1914. There were shortcuts taken during the original construction that resulted in some

McKinley's Blue Anchor Restaurant at Pennypack Circle, which ended four-lane traffic at the time this picture was taken in 1933.

parts of the road only having four lanes. Political decisions by Sunny Jim McNichol and Tacony's Joseph Costello often changed the routes overnight. One such spot was located near Friends Hospital, where two bridges over train tracks along the route were just four lanes, making them impediments to traffic until they were enlarged to twelve lanes in 1939. The cost of construction was $3.5 million, and upon completion the road was named Northeast Boulevard. In 1918, it was renamed in honor of Theodore Roosevelt, giving it the name we use today. In 1926, the United States initiated the interstate highway system that established federal "US" routes. Roosevelt Boulevard became part of Route 1 (US 1), the first interstate highway in the nation.

Once completed to Pennypack Circle, the streets department announced a new driving pattern for the boulevard. Trucks and buses were required to use the outside lanes and cars the inner lanes. Despite this change, the American Automobile Club, after inspecting the boulevard between Oxford and Pennypack Circles, announced that it had two flaws that made it unsafe. First, the city had not provided proper lighting or installed necessary traffic lights. There was only one red light at Cottman Street, making this entire section of road a speedway. Second, the boulevard's eleven-foot side grass plots with trees (to prevent glare from cars going the other way) and its eighty-foot center grass plot made for conditions in which pedestrians would "find crossing a hazardous procedure." The red light condition was corrected, but nothing was done to improve the ability of pedestrians to cross the boulevard.

As Mayor Ahbridge had predicted, Roosevelt Boulevard became a favorite Sunday ride for Philadelphians in the 1920s. Several restaurants opened around Pennypack Circle, above which the boulevard narrowed to two lanes. For some time, this was considered the end of the boulevard. Felin's Hot Dog Stand, McKinley's Blue Anchor Restaurant and Townsend's Barbeque Restaurant were all located at Pennypack Circle. The most popular of these was owned by "Josh" Townsend, who featured barbecued Virginia baked ham and chicken. By the early 1930s, Townsend's Barbeque was widely known in the area for having good food. Josh's son, Bud, worked in the restaurant until he got married and started his own business. Bud knew of a small restaurant at Red Lion Road and Roosevelt Boulevard located across the street from Roosevelt Airport. When it became available, his father helped him rent the building so he could start his own business. Bud built an addition and divided the one large room downstairs to make two rooms. The addition contained beautiful pictures of modern 1930s airplanes. The room facing the airport was made into a soda and ice cream parlor for the many families with children that came to see the planes take off and land. The other side of the addition contained tables with tablecloths for those wishing to have a full, classy dinner. Although this stretch of the boulevard would not be widened for a number of years, Townsend's Airport Restaurant became a very popular spot for "Sunday drivers" in the 1930s. (As a youngster, Dr. Harry Silcox spent many a Sunday in the restaurant watching planes take off and land at Boulevard Airport.)

Its location directly across from the Boulevard Airport and near the Budd Company plant undoubtedly helped Townsend's become a successful northeast restaurant. Bud's wife, Ruth, served as the waitress while a hired cook prepared the food. A recent interview with their daughter, Alice Townsend Altman, reveals a great deal about this famous gathering place. Alice grew up in the second floor of the restaurant. There were eight rooms in which the family lived above the restaurant: a living room, a bathroom, three bedrooms and a playroom for toys. The remaining rooms were used to store food for the restaurant. There was no kitchen on the second floor, so each

A 1940 picture of the Townsend Airport Restaurant at Red Lion Road and Roosevelt Boulevard at the site of the Boulevard Airport. Alice Townsend Altman, Bud Townsend's six-year-old daughter, is standing in front of the restaurant.

morning after she dressed, Alice had to go outside and then into the restaurant entrance, where her mother cooked breakfast. The bus ride to Jacobs School took well over an hour since there were so many single farm stops needed to pick up children in the Bustleton area. Later, she would attend Frankford High and then transfer to Lincoln High, from which she graduated in 1952. While it was unconventional, Alice loved her home atop the restaurant because she was near the airport and able to play on the airport grounds. In the 1930s, airplanes were new and exciting. It was a wonderful life to meet pilots from all over the United States and to see all of the different kinds of airplanes that used the airport. Alice and her brother took the back bedrooms of the second floor so that they could see the planes take off and land while waiting to fall asleep.

All of this came quickly to an end in 1942 when World War II gas rationing halted "Sunday driving," and the government closed Boulevard Airport as a security measure. Suddenly, there was no business at the restaurant, forcing Alice's father to close it and take a defense job at Budd Company. The family moved to Mayfair at this time. After the war, the restaurant reopened under new management and became Ye Old Ale House in 1946; it remained a restaurant under different names until 2008, when it was demolished, with a Starbucks and a Verizon office now erected on the site.

"Josh" Townsend and his sons at his restaurant at Pennypack Circle. His son, Bud Townsend, later ran the airport restaurant at Red Lion and Roosevelt Boulevard.

Work continued on the boulevard to widen the road and enlarge bridges to provide for twelve lanes of traffic. The last construction job before World War II was done between Oxford Circle and Pennypack Circle to complete the original plans and make that nine-lane portion into twelve lanes. Unlike other roads in the northeast—such as those in Tacony made with sandstone from the Disston factory as a base or the famous cemented "Crossan" Streets in Burholme not built to the city's specifications by contractor Kennedy Crossan—the boulevard was completed with the modern equipment of the day. Pictures of workmen expanding the boulevard with such equipment appeared in the local papers in 1937.

After World War II, the extension of the twelve-lane boulevard was completed to the city line at Bucks County. Little consideration was given to the earlier complaints about the flaws of the boulevard, however. As the population of the northeast exploded in the postwar period, and builders developed land as quickly as they could buy it, the traffic patterns worsened. By the turn of the twenty-first century, the boulevard had become infamous for the perils it presented. In 2001, State Farm Insurance Company published its annual report on America's ten most dangerous intersections. Rankings were determined by the number of accidents at an intersection, how many people were injured and the number of cars in the accidents. Two intersections on Roosevelt Boulevard were on the list: Red Lion Road and Grant Avenue, numbers two and three, respectively. The days of a leisurely drive to Boulevard Airport at Red Lion Road in the 1930s were long gone. Conditions got so bad that in 2002 the City of Philadelphia installed new street signs and in 2004 placed cameras on the intersections to catch speeders and those running the lights. In 2008, timers were installed to warn pedestrians of how much time they had left to cross the street before the light changed. How effective these methods will be has yet to be determined. It is ironic that the cost of these safety measures—over $3 million—was the same as the original 1903 Torresdale Boulevard project from Broad Street to Pennypack Circle. One wonders if there will ever be enough money to provide for a safe boulevard and if the flaws announced in the newspapers in 1937 that have remained uncorrected for over seventy years will still be with us seventy years from now.

***

GOODBYE TO THE HORSE AND BUGGY

A study of the census in 1900 reveals that there were three thousand horses in Philadelphia, most of them located in the farm regions of Northeast Philadelphia. The main method of transportation from farm to farm was by horse or carriage. By 1910, that figure had been reduced to less that two thousand horses due to the growth of the automobile. The minutes of the Holmesburg Improvement Association are filled with complaints by horse owners of having their animal frightened by cars racing through town. Holmesburg had always depended on horses to provide jobs for the town folks. The blacksmiths located originally in Holmesburg had moved out of town to Linden and Frankford Avenues, still keeping many a horse shoed and carriage repaired. Suddenly, these shops were becoming gas stations, and horses were seen less frequently visiting them. A number of citizens got together in Holmesburg to discuss the problem of owning horses and the increased number of cars on the road. Most of the people attending the meeting were horse

One of the largest horse shows held in the northeast was at Welsh Road and Roosevelt Boulevard in 1934. This picture shows the LuLu Temple Honor Guard in the center of the jumping area. Six thousand people attended this event, stopping traffic on the Boulevard for hours.

lovers who wanted to keep their horses and have a safe space provided for them to ride.

In 1918, the newly organized Pennypack Riding Club of Holmesburg petitioned the City of Philadelphia for a bridle path next to the Pennypack Creek. The organization was formed by the horse lovers of the community who wanted to provide a safe area where horsemen could ride without interference from cars. The petition was granted by the city, and a fourteen-mile bridle path opened on September 15 the same year. The club was composed of devotees of horseback riding from the northeast section of the city. The charter said that the purpose of this new organization was to promote and encourage horsemanship and other equestrian skills. Subscribers signing the original charter application were Chancellor Day, 3504 Rhawn Street; L.A. Dowling, 4664 Wyoming Street; Ray George, 6883 Algard Street; and Wright Bryan, 9610 Banes Street. The bridle path next to the Pennypack Creek seemed the answer to rider safety. A second mandate of the charter was to provide the community with examples of equestrian skills, which they interpreted as providing horse shows where horse and rider could exhibit horsemanship for the community.

Given the new city restrictions on horses, this took some time to finalize. However, in 1930 a charter was given to the Pennypack Riding Club to conduct horse shows. The charter was signed by President Judge J. Willis

Female competition in the horse jumping event at Pennypack Riding Club held at Welsh Road and the Boulevard in 1934.

Martin in Common Pleas Court No. 5, the man who also incorporated the Pennypack Riding Club of Holmesburg at the same time. The same year, the Pennypack Riding Club put on its first horse show at the north end of the Pennypack Bridge on Roosevelt Boulevard. Proceeds of the event went to fund Frankford Hospital, with all prizes at the event funded by friends of the hospital. In all, there were ninety entries competing in thirty-three classes of competition. Miss Cartwright of Beth Ayers received three silver cups and four blue ribbons when she and her horse were judged the best in saddle. A crowd of three thousand traveled past Pennypack Circle to see the horse show on the open fields above the Pennypack Creek Bridge.

The largest event ever sponsored by the Pennypack Riding Club was Pennypack Park Day on October 23, 1933. Celebrations on that day were organized by business and civic groups and took place along the fourteen-mile bridle path next to the Pennypack Creek. The grand prize of the day went to Evergreen Farms for having the most riders in the parade, twenty-four. The participants gathered at Bustleton and Castor Avenues at 1:00 p.m. and formed lines of horses that gradually winded their way to the bridle path receiving stand beneath the Roosevelt Boulevard Bridge. This equestrian pageant resulted in a parade of one hundred horses riding through the park. The parade was led by the historic Torresdale Tally-Ho four-horse carriage, which carried judges and honored guests. Near the reviewing stands, well-known riders staged demonstrations of correct riding skills for the gathering crowds. These events were sponsored by the Northeast Chamber of Commerce

Hackney Tally-Ho horse carriage transports the judges for the 1933 Pennypack Park Day beneath Roosevelt Boulevard on the bridle path near the creek.

and the Riding Club of Pennypack. The crowds at the events of the day were estimated to be over ten thousand people strong.

The Pennypack Riding Club was becoming an organization that worked well with charities to raise money. In 1934, they put on a Cripple Child Benefit horse show for Shriners Hospital at Welsh Road and Roosevelt Boulevard. The boulevard had to be closed off for the day when well over six thousand people jammed the intersection to see the show. There were a number of spills and thrills that day in the difficult four-foot jumping event. In all, there were seventeen events and over one hundred contestants entered. Interspersed during the races were performances by the LuLu Temple Drill Team and a concert band with a choir. The final parade featured horses and the LuLu Temple Legion of Honor marching into the twilight, a thrilling climactic effect to end the benefit show that received a standing ovation from the crowd. One year later, a spring horse show at the same location proudly announced the Eighth Annual Horse Show sponsored by the Pennypack Riding Club of Northeast Philadelphia. Northeast Philadelphia maintained its support for Pennypack Riding Club's horse shows throughout the 1930s.

Yet another club was formed to promote horse shows and equestrian events. Adopting the name the Pennypack Country Club in 1921 and led by President Albert Herning, it purchased the old Barton mansion at Welsh and Willits Roads. The building was in poor condition, having been a former girls' boarding school. The country club gutted the interior of the building and constructed ultramodern interior rooms to make it into an up-to-date country club. The twenty-one acres of ground on the property also featured a landing field for airplanes and open space. But there was no golf course like the one at nearby Frankford-Torresdale Country Club. The lack of a golf course was a great disadvantage for the Pennypack Country Club because it limited the club's activities and its future income. Nevertheless, Albert Herning accepted leadership of the group, proposing that several horse shows be planned for the next season. One year later, Kyle Dudley accepted the office of president, Fred Woerner became vice-president and Max R. Leven treasurer as the organization elected new leaders. These leaders tabled the proposed horse shows to further provide services for their members at the country club headquarters.

The Pennypack Country Club was in financial trouble from the beginning. While it wanted to be active in civic improvements in the

Riders at the Western Show sponsored by the Pennypack Country Club in 1939.

community, it took all of its resources to keep the building open for members. The country club was very popular in the summers, featuring picnic lunches on the grounds with a place to go in case of rain. For all of these reasons, it was not until 1939 that members held their first horse show. On August 8 of that year, they held the "Northeast Horse Show" at the Pennypack Country Club. The show was to benefit the Park Guard Pension Fund and featured the Park Guards of the City of Philadelphia in formation and trick riding. The public was invited to enter the western-style riding competition that featured imitations of riding in movies. The event attracted seven thousand spectators and was deemed a success by the country club.

The final horse show conducted by any club in Pennypack Park or nearby was held in 1943. The war limited the number of riders available because most eligible men were off to war. Sponsored by the Pennypack Country Club, the show consisted of a card of twenty events with eighty-five participants. Many of them were young boys. The competition had the popular four-foot jumping event, but when only six hundred spectators showed up, the country club decided to review its policy of sponsoring horse shows. Financial difficulties and declining interest led to the end of horse shows after World War II.

By the late 1960s, there were few horse stables near Holmesburg or Pennypack Park. Today, an occasional rider can be found on the bridle paths above Pine Road, where a few small stables are located; however, horsemanship and shows are no longer part of the scene in lower Northeast Philadelphia. Nevertheless, many horse lovers, remembering family tradition, still live in the area.

***

FROM CREEKS TO PUBLIC POOLS

The earliest histories of Philadelphia describe how those living in the city relied on the Delaware River. Commerce was one of the city's main businesses, and the river was where it happened. Rowboats and small craft roamed the river in the summer as many locals fished and swam. It was not surprising when Northeast Philadelphia became populated that communities like Tacony and Torresdale became popular swimming locations. Farmers from Bustleton, Burholme, Byberry and beyond vacationed at Tacony's Buttermilk tavern to swim and fish in the summer months. John Risdon's Ferry opened up the beauties of New Jersey by way of the Rancocas Creek, offering summer vacations in small towns along the creek. Many center city residents began taking the steamboat north to enjoy the natural beauty of the location. Given these attractions of the Delaware River, it was not surprising that public swimming beaches were established along the river.

By 1900, swimmers increasingly used the riverbanks for swimming. Even in communities like Northern Liberties and Kensington, not known for their clean water, there were hundreds of swimmers in the river. In Northeast Philadelphia, Linden Avenue and the Delaware River was a popular spot used by swimmers until local leaders became concerned about safety and how many swimmers were removing their clothes to swim. The lewdness offended the sensibilities of local citizens. A movement led by businessman T. Kilby Smith Jr. (1871–1945), president of the Torresdale Improvement Association; N. Edwin Lindell, president of the Wissinoming Improvement Association;

William Boal of the Holmesburg Businessmen Association; and James F. Gossner, president of the Pleasant Hill Improvement Association, prompted a request to Mayor J. Hampton Moore to consider a public city beach at Pleasant Hill. Moore agreed, signing into law a provision for a public beach in the northeast on the Delaware River in 1917.

Planning for the beach included a cleanup program to remove debris and rocks from one thousand feet of shoreline at Point Pleasant. Sand was placed along the riverbank to make it look like the New Jersey Shore. A gazebo for shade was built above the riverbank for spectators with a first-aid station next to it and portable toilet facilities in the rear. Final preparations included a ten- by twenty-five-square-foot raft with a water ladder, chained to the river bottom, twenty feet offshore. By July 1917, the beach was ready for the opening-day ceremonies.

Local leader T. Kilby Smith Jr. spoke for the community at the opening ceremonies, followed by the main speaker of the day, Mayor J. Hampton Moore. Moore, who had a summer home in Torresdale, told the crowd that bathers could "not use trees and beaches to hide when they changed their clothes." Moore then warned female bathers "that unnecessary display of dimpled knees will be met with correction by policeman." He finished by saying that Pleasant Hill will be "a model for ladies and gentleman of the Northeast." The mayor's concern for the new beach was clear—lewdness would not be tolerated and the Victorian values of the time would be upheld.

Archie Boyd was relieved of his duties as a policeman on the parkway in Philadelphia and placed in charge of Torresdale's beach area. He was a brute of a man, standing six feet, two inches and weighing 220 pounds. After being introduced by the mayor, Boyd reinforced Moore's statements, "I am not going to stand for any undressed Lizzies sitting around on my sandy beaches." Also hired was George Kiathler, swim instructor at the University of Pennsylvania. He and five assistants were to be available each day along the beach to teach swimming.

One of the problems Boyd faced was that the six roomy tents to be used as dressing rooms had not arrived. They were gifts from the U.S. Army but were delayed by the needs of the upcoming war. Therefore, the beach opened without them. This led to swimmers using cars to change into swimming attire. Mayor Moore sent additional policeman to Pleasant Hill to stop this practice. However, the tents came in 1919, and the 1921 picture of the beach shows them being used by beachgoers. Under Boyd,

Pleasant Hill beach in Torresdale 1921. Note the tent changing areas on the right and the gazebo on the left as guards patrol in a rowboat.

Fish kill in the Delaware near Pleasant Hill public swimming beach in 1935.

Pleasant Hill Beach soon became the most popular swimming spot for over a decade in Northeast Philadelphia.

However, by the late 1920s, the Delaware River began to show the effects of the industrial age. Oil, now a major necessity for the manufacturing plants along the river, found its way into the river. Whether manufacturers were naïve to the properties of oil or just careless, large quantities of oil appeared on the surface of the river. Large fish kills now occurred, often taking weeks to clean and remove the smelly dead fish from the shores. This eventually caused the city to close the Pleasant Hill beach in the 1930s.

The largest remaining swim area with clean water was the Pennypack Creek. It had always been used by local communities for swimming and other activities. The creek had been used as a baptismal site prior to 1871 by the Holmesburg Baptist Church. Before 1871, the spot used for most immersions was located above the falls west of Frankford Avenue, where the church conducted twelve baptisms per year in the creek. The last immersion was in 1928, when Reverend MacDonald held services on the Pennypack Creek to celebrate the 100th anniversary of the church.

In planning the swimming areas on Pennypack Creek, the city decided to use the enlarged water areas created by the old dams left from the

Pennypack Park swimming area located under the Roosevelt Boulevard Bridge. Unlike other swimming locations, it had a diving board, making it a very popular spot.

1830 industrial age of the creek. The water was deep at these places and provided five to six feet in which to swim.

The city provided support services to the Pennypack beaches similar to those formerly at Pleasant Hill. Available to the public were portable changing areas, portable toilets and lifeguards. The city added additional park guards to discourage swimmers who tried to swim in unsupervised areas. The fine for violators was $12.50 for each infraction. A third infraction resulted in parents being called and told to pick their child up at the Park Guard Station next to the boulevard.

Mayfair resident Charles Farrell, who grew up in Holmesburg, still remembers swimming in the Pennypack Creek. As a kid he swam in all of the sites near Holmesburg. He recalled their locations near the falls

Smitty's swim area located on the falls by the Rhawn Street Bridge; it was at times used illegally by the community at night, using car lights to illuminate the swim area.

of the Rowland Shovel Works and the Hartel's Calico Print Works (torn down) by the Rhawn Street Bridge. In all there were four swimming areas in Holmesburg, each with names given to them by the kids of that day. Kingies' was behind Pennypack woods, Smitty's near Rhawn Street where the first-aid stand was located (near where the music pavilion is today), Ammon's on the creek behind the old poorhouse building and Boulevard where the creek crossed Roosevelt Boulevard. The most populated of these sites was Smitty's, where there was a food stand, as well as an open spring where water was available from the historical Crystal Springs fountain. The Crystal Spring plantation house of Colonel James Lewis had been torn down in the early 1900s when the city purchased the land for the park, but the reputation for pure water from Crystal Springs still attracted many to the site.

These same swimming areas were used at night, although it was unlawful. On extremely hot nights, the Rhawn Street entrance near the falls of the old print works was filled with cars entering the park after 10:00 p.m. The cars were parked facing the Pennypack with their headlights left on to illuminate the swim area above the falls. Although the city had regulations against this practice, hot nights nevertheless produced hundreds of people trying to get relief from the evening heat.

There were some problems with these swimming areas. While the water was evaluated each day for bacteria counts, these tests were not accurate since the Pennypack was a fast-moving stream and water counts changed continuously. On many days, certain areas were closed. On other days, large storms increased the number of tree branches and debris in the creek and caused the water to be muddy. The mud didn't matter to most swimmers, but large logs in the water required swimmers to listen for the guards' warning whistles. Another hazard along the Pennypack Creek was the trestle railroad bridge west of Frankford Avenue. For the daredevils of the day, manhood required that you jump from the trestle into the creek. There were two dangers involved: first was to be sure to land in deep water, and second was to avoid oncoming trains that ran on schedule between Holmesburg and Bustleton.

The building of the Boulevard Pools in 1929 and the 1930s construction of a city bathhouse at State Road and Levick Street led to many swimmers going to these locations. On weekends, many swimmers went to the far northeast areas of Somerton Pools and Highway Pools at the city limits on the Roosevelt Boulevard, where new swimming pools had opened. However, these pools had an entrance price of fifty cents, a sum that few kids had during the Depression. Another choice was to go to the newly built city bathhouses. The nearest was located on State Road next to the Tacony Palmyra Bridge. It was organized by hourly swims, with Monday and Wednesday being girls' days and Tuesday and Thursday being boys' days. Friday was kept open for special events. This limited access to the city pools caused many children to use the Pennypack swimming areas that were free and always open.

There was one other factor that encouraged kids to stay away from the Pennypack Creek. In the 1940s, the battle against polio was at its height. The March of Dimes campaigns initiated in the 1930s by Theodore Roosevelt emphasized that children should not swim during the "polio season," which began in late August. Newspapers were filled with daily stories about children getting polio. Increasingly, public pools were built in the northeast, and the contamination in the Pennypack Creek continued to increase as more homes were built in the upper northeast. By the 1960s, the idea of having a swimming area in the Pennypack was considered unhealthy and dangerous, ending the era of swimming in rivers and creeks of Northeast Philadelphia. The expansion of public pools followed in Philadelphia after World War II.

CHAPTER 5

NEW HOMES AND FRESH FACES

***

CASTING A NEW LIGHT ON CASTOR AVENUE

In writing articles about Northeast Philadelphia, one is continually finding individuals who were often ignored by historians but who were indispensible to the development of a specific section of the city. One such person was Hyman Korman, who was born in Lithuania in 1903 and lived his early life in a farmhouse near what is today Oxford Circle on Roosevelt Boulevard. He came to America in 1924 to study railroading, which at the time was very lucrative business. Philadelphia was home to the Pennsylvania Railroad, then the mightiest railroad of them all. However, Korman never got a job with the "Pennsy," having to settle for work in women's apparel in the textile industry. Like many Jewish immigrants in America, he married soon after securing his job. To save money, he moved in with his in-laws in a farmhouse near where Oxford Circle is now.

The northeast in 1910 was populated by farmers who cherished their independence and wanted to be left alone. Many of them opposed the Consolidation Act of 1854, which brought their farms

In the 1930s, houses were built in the Oxford Circle area, most of them residential row homes. These Elbridge Street homes are an attempt by Hyman Korman to break the monotony of the row home by changing the roof design every second house.

into the city, and resisted sending their children to public schools. In 1926, when Korman lived in Oxford Circle, it remained a rural area of a city. The census for that time showed 500 automobiles, 4,000 cows, 3,000 horses and 2,500 pigs for Northeast Philadelphia. Korman's living on the farm near Oxford Circle was unique and different from the experience of most Jewish immigrants, who were crowded together in poor housing in South Philadelphia.

Living in Northeast Philadelphia left the Korman family with few Jewish neighbors; in fact, the census indicates that there were more blacks than Jews living in the northeast. Jewish historian Maxwell Whiteman describes the nearest Jewish settlement to Korman as being two miles away in Port Richmand, below Frankford Creek on William Street. He describes this area as being the "first exclusively Jewish Street in Philadelphia." Yehzekiel Bernstein, a Polish immigrant, was its first settler. Nevertheless, Korman was quite comfortable living and raising his children in the northeast. Korman's sons were born on the farm, Max William in 1906 and Samuel in 1909, and as boys they were forced to do farm chores. A newspaper account in 1962 said of Max, "The firm grip he displays proudly today came from years of milking cows."

In 1914, an event occurred that changed the makeup of Northeast Philadelphia and Hyman Korman's life forever. A seven-mile stretch of Roosevelt Boulevard was open to traffic to Pennypack Circle. The new highway went right through the farm on which Hyman Korman had lived. Korman immediately understood that this extension would raise land values in the northeast and encourage residential development. Korman was well positioned to take advantage of the situation. He had previously purchased land in the area predicting a residential growth of homes. He had purchased the Hamilton Farm in 1917 at what is now Castor and Devereaux Streets and one year later bought the Dawson Farm at Castor and Magee Street. Both of these farms were purchased at very low prices in a time when property values were low. Using these properties as a basis for a loan, Hyman Korman organized a building company and partnered with Alfred Orleans real estate and insurance company and began building homes in the northeast.

Korman and Orleans's first homes were built in 1924 on Oakley Street south of Levick Street and along Martin's Mill Road near the Cheltenham Township line in what is now Lawndale. Soon after these construction jobs were finished, A.P. Orleans left Korman and began his own company. Both Hyman Korman and Alfred Orleans then started to groom their sons to eventually take over their businesses. In the decades that followed, they remained friends as they competed to build homes throughout the northeast.

The early homes built by Korman were purchased by gentile families. There was an unofficial agreement among the builders of the day that Jews could not purchase homes in the northeast. Marvin Orleans was quoted in 1964 saying that "had Korman and Orleans not been Jewish, I think they would have run their jobs restricted to gentile buyers. They were not too crazy about selling to Jews for fear of what it would do to their gentile market." Nevertheless, Korman began selling to Jewish families.

It wasn't until the 1930s when Jewish families begin to move into new homes in the northeast on Castor Avenue. Hyman Korman's sales agent in the 1920s was Alex Burchuk, himself a Russian Jewish immigrant. Burchuk's son, Aaron, who took over the business after his father died, was instrumental in selling new homes to Jews who wished to move into the Oxford Circle/Castor Avenue area. An example of their sales brochure remains for us to read: "Hyman Korman's air conditioned-insulated-oil burning homes. Built on lots 20 feet by 81.6 feet, the house has three large airy bedrooms, two tiled baths and rock lath plastering throughout. The house has a modern spacious kitchen with breakfast room with plenty of closet space. Price $5,490. Similar homes with two bedrooms on Devereaux Street for $3,390." These homes were all located on the site of the old Hamilton Farm Hyman Korman's first acquisition in the northeast.

By the 1950s, Hyman Korman Homes Inc. had developed a fine reputation for quality and fair dealings with the public. An article written about him at the time observed that "Korman has his own code of wisdom when it comes to building. His success in the field has been the result of good judgment, and his fortunate position of also being a 'cash buyer,' paying on delivery for his building materials, enables him to buy large quantities at favorable prices."

Once the Oxford Circle area was filled with homes, the builders pushed farther north. A pattern then developed in which Roosevelt Boulevard became the dividing line between the Jewish community on the west and the large Irish, Italian and German Catholic area to the east. There was endless speculation as to why these neighborhood patterns had occurred; many cited the fact that Hyman Korman's farm was located on the west side and that A.P. Orleans had also started to build there soon after. Asked to explain these ethnic groupings caused by this unofficial dividing line, Marvin Orleans (who died in September 1986) responded, "I guess that was because of the start we had already made west of the Boulevard. The Jewish people felt more comfortable. I think it goes back to feeling comfortable." Ironically, although Korman and Orleans were responsible for the growth of the Jewish neighborhoods along Castor Avenue, Hyman Korman did not become part of this neighborhood. Korman built a home for his wife and himself at 4901 Oxford Avenue in predominantly Protestant Frankford, east of Roosevelt Boulevard, and was living there until his death in 1970 at age eighty-eight.

It is clear from the story of Hyman Korman that most of the Jewish families that settled in Northeast Philadelphia in the years after World War II moved into the area because of the opportunity presented by Korman selling homes that were open to Jews. Jewish families at the time were moving from Strawberry mansion, Logan, Olney and South Philadelphia into the Oxford Circle/Castor Avenue section. Many were children of the working-class eastern European immigrants who had never owned a home. They were shopkeepers, salesman, city employees, factory workers and clerks. They were also lawyers, accountants and schoolteachers. They opened delicatessens and stores along Castor Avenue, making it the Jewish shopping area until Lit Brother's and Roosevelt Mall opened at Cottman and Castor Avenue in the early 1960s. Many policemen moved into the northeast, and one longtime resident, Morton Solomon, became president of his synagogue and the city's first police commissioner. Parades and events for the neighborhood usually ended at Temple Sholom near Oxford Circle, then the most influential and powerful synagogue in the Castor Avenue area.

The houses in the area remain the same, but the neighborhood is in the process of changing to accommodate yet another generation of immigrants. A newly arrived Asian and Brazilian population has developed in the last decade. Many of the old Jewish stores have closed, replaced by many new ethic stores that cater to these new populations. Nevertheless, to understand the founding of the community one must begin with Hyman Korman.

Much of this information came from Peter Binzen's article about the northeast found in Murray Friedman's book Philadelphia Jewish Life 1940–2000.

✳✳✳

Welcoming Rhawnhurst

The history of Rhawnhurst is more easily understood after studying the history of Castor Avenue below Cottman Avenue, built by Hyman Korman. Rhawnhurst developed directly out of the events that shaped the growth of the Castor Avenue/Oxford Circle section. In 1950, building along Castor Avenue reached Cottman Street, above which was a small dirt road that wandered into Fox Chase. The area was named for the Fox Chase Inn, a 1705 hotel used by fox hunters in colonial times. They often traveled from center city Philadelphia to hunt. Composed of farmland and open fields, the small village

A view of Castor Avenue below Rhawn Street in 1950. There are few houses in this rural area.

remained the center of hunting activity and a gentleman's retreat well into the twentieth century.

Many historic structures are still intact throughout Fox Chase. The Verree House on Verree Road was the site of a raid by British troops during the Revolutionary War. Only a foundation exists there today. Fox Chase farm is the only remaining active farm in Philadelphia County with many of its original buildings and is used exclusively by the Philadelphia School District. Fox Chase began as a land grant from William Penn to Lord Stanley and then passed to the McVeigh family for over two hundred years. Besides these land grants, the ancestor of Humphrey Waterman of Holmesburg, also named Humphrey, came from Barbados to Pennsylvania in 1698 and purchased 1,100 acres of land in Fox Chase. This land was held for years and never developed as farmland, keeping it an ideal hunting area.

When the Fox Chase area was finally broken up into smaller tracts of land in the nineteenth century, many later houses were built in the area. Left from these building days are two of Philadelphia's most notable historic mansions: Ryerss mansion in Burholme and Knowlton mansion, designed by Frank Furness in Fox Chase.

144

These large blocks of land began to be broken up into smaller parcels in the 1860s. The first change occurred when Robert W. Ryerss died in 1859, leaving his summer home Burholme and land to the local community to be used as a museum and park. The local community was so grateful that they named their town Burholme and thus made it separate from Fox Chase.

A second major neighborhood name change took place when the building of homes reached Cottman Street in the 1950s. The name changing of the area above Cottman Street on Castor Avenue was instigated by a group of real estate men that included A.P. Orleans. The name Fox Chase to them stood for the old community, and what they wanted was to build a new community with wide, modern streets, new-styled homes and new schools. Following a private discussion by the real estate operators, the decision was made to advertise the newly built homes as being in Rhawnhurst. The name was derived from two former Fox Chase bankers, George Washington Rhawn and William H. Rhawn, both of whom had spent their lives improving the financial and civic life of Fox Chase. In 1860, George had petitioned the state senate to operate the Fox Chase railroad. While the bill passed, the Civil War broke out, putting the project on hold until after the war. Nevertheless, George opened the First Charter Bank of Fox Chase, which became the major financial institution in the area for the next one hundred years. In his lifetime, George Rowen wrote only one book, *A Move for Better Roads: Essays on Road Making and Maintenance and Road Laws*. William Rhawn was the president of the National Bank of the Republic in the 1870s, following in George's footsteps.

In 1879, William Rhawn decided to build a summer home in Fox Chase at a cost of $37,386.16 for the land and building. In what turned out to be the most valuable asset in his building plan, Rhawn hired architect Frank Furness to design the building at a cost of $600.00. Today, the building is a nationally recognized historic site and is admired by all because it was designed by the now famous Frank Furness. William's wife, Hettie Rhawn, named the building Knowlton after her great-grandfather John Knowles's manor house in England. The city named the road in front of Knowlton "Rhawn" Street because William Rhawn paid for the city to pave the distance between the new house and the city's established streets. Rhawn died in 1899, but the street name remained, only to be resurrected by real estate entrepreneurs sixty years later.

A pre–Civil War stable still located at Castor and Bustleton Avenues on Pegasus Riding Academy grounds.

The Fox Chase connection was played down by the real estate lobby and the newness of the section highlighted. Through the intervention of the real estate lobby, a school was built in 1955 on Castor Avenue that the real estate lobby and community insisted on calling the Rhawnhurst Elementary School. The building of the Northeast Regional Library on Cottman Street further enhanced the appeal of the neighborhood. These new institutions, like the twin homes built by A.P. Orleans, greatly enhanced Rhawnhust's salability.

Before 1940, when the area was part of Fox Chase, there were many stables in Rhawnhurst near Pennypack Park that rented horses for riding in the park. A major stable was located at Bell's Corner, Castor Avenue and Rhawn Street. A large horse stable barn built prior to the Civil War is still located on the property, a reminder to all of the horse riding that took place in the area. The barn is part of Pegasus Riding Academy and is used when they have an overflow of horses. The Pegasus Riding Academy "provides disabled individuals with therapeutic activity" on horseback, using the fourteen horses now stabled there. This remains the lone artifact to the once famous 1920–40 era of horse shows in Northeast Philadelphia.

Over time, the growth of residential housing on Castor Avenue to Cottman Street directly connected this newly developing area to Oxford Circle and away from Fox Chase. The baby boom after World War II increased demand for housing, which continued into the 1960s. With the intervention of the real estate lobby, the area became bound to the developments along Castor Avenue. The opening of the Lit Brothers Store and the malls along Cottman Street greatly enhanced the area as a new residential community. As many stores closed along the Castor Avenue/Oxford Circle area, and the row homes with small streets in the area below Cottman Street became less popular as a place to live, Rhawnhurst became one of the most attractive residential locations because of its new housing stock design. Most Rhawnhurst homes were twins along with some ranchers and duplexes built on wider streets by local builder A.P. Orleans. The homes in Rhawnhurst were more expensive, but residents of lower Castor Avenue still moved to Rhawnhurst for a better standard of living. Rhawnhurst continued to spread into the area once called Fox Chase. Rhawnhurst today encompasses zip codes 19152 and 19111. The geographical center of Rhawnhurst is the intersection of Castor Avenue and Rhawn Street. Besides the Baptist, Lutheran, Presbyterian and Episcopal protestant churches of the region there were also many Jewish congregations, including Ahavas Torah, Beth Medrash Harav, B'nai Israel–Ohev Zedek, the Lubavitch Center, Net Zedek Ezrath Israel, Ohr Somayach and Congregation Mesilat Yesharim.

Rhawnhurst residents of note besides the Rhawn brothers are difficult to name. Because it is an area that developed recently, few of its inhabitants have become well known. However, athletes like Billy "Pickles" Kennedy, recently killed in an auto accident in Florida, was a northeast legend when he played on Temple University's 1958 Final Four team, and politician Brett Mandel, a recent candidate for the office of city controller in Philadelphia, both attended the Rhawnhurst Elementary School. Many young people have moved out of the neighborhood, leaving senior citizens to be serviced by Rhawnhurst NORC, an organization that helps seniors to remain independent and in their homes. It is still a changing neighborhood, like so many communities in Philadelphia today.

***

UNITING THE AFRICAN AMERICAN COMMUNITY

As the previous article on the history of African Americans in Northeast Philadelphia demonstrated, there were strong connections and a great deal of interaction between the various black communities of the area. Still, each community had its own identity. This was due in large measure to the way black churches north of Frankford were formed. As the black community grew in Tacony, so too did its desire for a church. Most influential in this movement were the Vaughn, Scott, Whitmore, Rice and Booker families. Initially, prayer meetings were held in homes until money was raised to rent a hall at Longshore Street and State Road in 1919. Religious traditions brought by these families from Rice and Remington, Virginia, dictated that the church would be of Southern Baptist denomination. The church was named Star of Hope Baptist Church, and first pastor Reverend Philpot began services in 1920. By 1921, the church had purchased the old Holy Innocents Church as a permanent home.

In Holmesburg, legend has it that Reverend Andrew Jones (1854–1934) came to Northeast Philadelphia in 1896 to preach to blacks. He went to the Holmesburg Quarry located between the black settlement of Guinea Hill and Holmesburg. The quarry employed two hundred workers, 80 percent of whom were black. At its peak, 1896 to 1925, it was the largest employer of blacks in the northeast. After a few prayer meetings, he organized a Sunday school at the site. Within one year, Reverend John Boyd joined him and organized the Mount Zion Baptist Church in an old building on the grounds of the quarry. In 1900, Amos Shallcross gave the church a lot on Rowland Avenue, and the first church was built in the 1920s. In 1940, Reverend W. Nix paid off the mortgage, and a new church was planned at its present location on Welsh Road. The church was opened in 1972 under Reverend R.J. Waller, a man who served the Holmesburg black community for decades.

Bethany AME Church, the oldest church north of Frankford, was established according to local folklore in 1817 near the Holme Circle/Ashton Road section that became known to blacks as "Guinea Hill." The

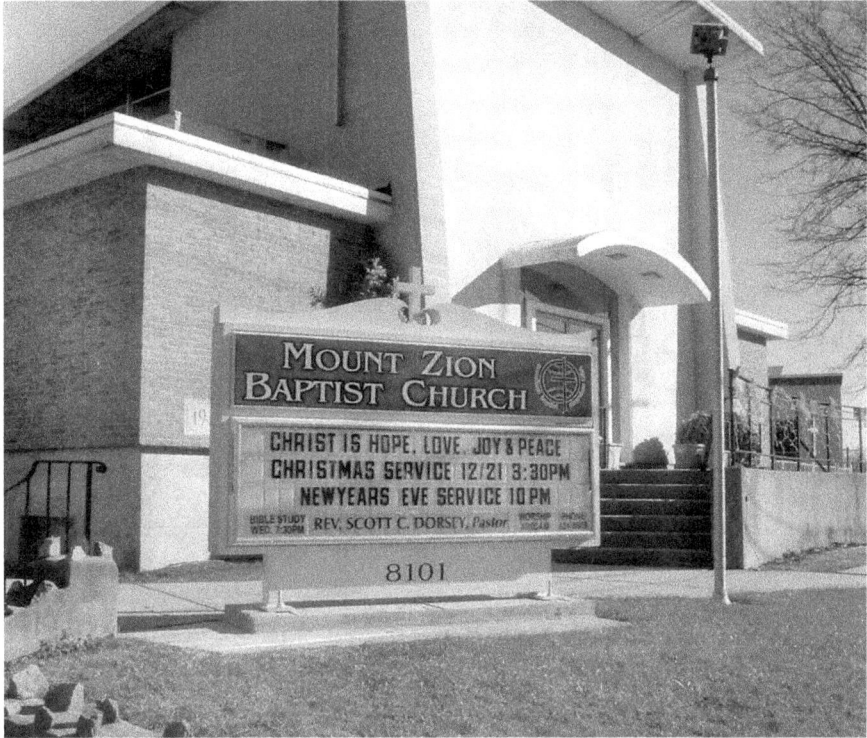

The largest black church in the northeast is the Mount Zion Baptist Church of Holmesburg.

name comes from the oral tradition of the black community that says the area was settled by free blacks from the West African nation of Guinea during the nineteenth century. The church building is still on the original site, but the famous black farming area and Holmesburg Quarry are long gone, victims of urbanization. None of these churches was connected or allied with churches in Frankford.

According to historian Samuel Willits, Guinea Hill dates back to before 1830, when some free Africans from Guinea settled there. They worked some small farms and established what was then a small population center. Also, jobs in local nursing homes and the Holmesburg Quarry were readily available. This became a stable black community that produced a number of important blacks in Northeast Philadelphia. An examination of the life of, one of its residents tells us much about what it was like to live there in the mid-twentieth century.

Miller Scott was well known to the people of Northeast Philadelphia, both white and black. During the Depression, Miller's father had

Holmesburg Quarry in the 1930s. Located across the street from Father Judge, the quarry once employed four hundred workers extracting stones for the walls of Holmesburg Prison. Of these workers, over 50 percent were black, and the quarry became the company with the largest number of black workers in Northeast Philadelphia.

purchased land in Guinea Hill while working for the WPA as a foreman on the construction of Byberry Hospital. It was the dream of many blacks to be able to have land so that they could develop small farms with their own chickens, pigs and goats. Scotty, as he was known, was educated at the white Jacobs School in Bustleton while living at Guinea Hill. Later, he attended Wilson Junior High School and then Northeast High School, which was then located at Eighth Street and Lehigh Avenue. A Polish boy named Eddie Karinski was Scotty's closest friend at Northeast High School and remained his lifelong friend. Scotty could recall few racial incidents in his youth, despite living in a white neighborhood.

He remembered the area well. There was a home for wayward children called St. Jerome's down Welsh Road (where the church is today) and behind it a horse stable called the Flying "A." From that point to the north of Rhawn Street there was nothing but open fields until you reached the Cottage Green Restaurant. A rest home for retired Bell Telephone operators could be found near where the intersection of Welsh Road and Holme Avenue is today. From Guinea

Hill to Roosevelt Boulevard there was just one big house owned by Samuel Stokes. Scotty knew everyone in the "Hill." Through the help of Republican leader Austin Meehan, he was appointed to a custodial position at Lincoln High School, a job he kept until his untimely death in 1990. He was respected and liked by all at Lincoln High School. He was remembered that same year with an assembly program and a special student award in his honor at graduation.

Bethany AME Church was an important institution in the Guinea Hill community. Founded with a connection to Mother Bethel AME Church at Sixth and Lombard Streets, it was at the time the only church available to African Americans living north of Frankford. In the later half of the century, the Stout and Carter families settled on tracts of land near the church. By the nineteenth century, Percy Carter was listed in *The Philadelphia Colored Directory* as one of the richest African Americans living in Northeast Philadelphia, despite the fact that he worked as a wagon driver at the Beale coal yards in Tacony. While stories from older blacks who knew the region insist that many blacks owned land in the region, maps for 1900 could only verify the Carter family land ownership. Richard C. Stout (1884–1958) was one of the most well-known blacks living on the "Hill." His weekend parties and gatherings of blacks from Frankford, Tacony and Holmesburg were events not to be missed. The food was unmatched, since it was taken directly from the cornfields, with freshly killed pigs and chickens from local black farms. These outings usually included the Floyd Booker, Theodore Heard and John Branch families.

Richard Stout's son Earl was destined to become the most powerful African American in Philadelphia in the 1980s. As the president of District 33 of the American Federation of State, County and Municipal Employees, Earl Stout represented all blue-collar workers in Philadelphia city government. Fellow union leader Joe Bloom called him "an extraordinary man, even when he was on his worst behavior." As a tough-talking union boss, Stout could and did influence mayoral elections in the city. In the process, he won unprecedented benefits for city workers. In the Guinea Hill neighborhood and throughout Northeast Philadelphia, Stout had the respect and admiration of most blacks. His house was often filled with members of the northeast black community seeking favors or city jobs. Earl Stout died of Alzheimer's disease at Mercy Suburban Hospital in Norristown after a long illness in 2006.

The civil rights movement of the 1960s and '70s gave the Northeast Philadelphia African American community new opportunities for job advancement and higher education. Some northeast African Americans emerged from this period as leaders, including many from the oldest black families of the area. Here are just a few.

From the Early family came Clark Early (nickname "Clarkie"), Northeast Philadelphia's first homegrown black lawyer. The Boston family's "Nootch" Boston became Philadelphia's first African American highway patrolman. The Collins family daughter, Caroline Collins, became the first African American girl to be admitted to St. Hubert's High School. Frank Fortson, one of Lincoln High School's greatest athletes, was among the first blacks in the country to be admitted to Princeton University on an athletic scholarship. The McIntosh family that lived on Welsh Road sent Lincoln High basketball star "Jimmy" McIntosh on to Villanova on a basketball scholarship to study government. Jim was not only a basketball star at Villanova but also went on to become an FBI agent in Chicago in the 1970s, and later he was the spokesperson for the FBI in Philadelphia. The Elliott family—led by Emma "Doll" Elliot, the organist, pianist and director of the Women's Day chorus at Mount Zion Church and the Ebenezer Church—sent their son Forrest Elliot to Lincoln High to become a football star. The Nix family produced Vivian Nix Early and Phenoris Nix (nicknamed "Phee"). Vivian graduated from Lincoln High and went on to major in psychology at the University of Pennsylvania in the 1970s and received her PhD from the University of Pennsylvania. Today she is a dean of graduate studies at Eastern University. Her sister Phenoris was active in local civic affairs and became director of a funeral home and an active church member, playing the violin and piano at services throughout the northeast.

It must also be noted that many of the men who grew up having partied at Guinea Hill enlisted en masse during the Vietnam War. Their service and valor rank with all who served from Northeast Philadelphia. Leon Brantley, who now lives in Frankford and is founder of the Historic and Patriotic Society of Northeast African Americans, can still recall the experiences of these men in Vietnam. After basic training at Fort Bragg, Virginia, Brantley proudly served his country in Vietnam until 1970, after which he returned home to Northeast Philadelphia. Among those from the area who served with Brantley were Wallace Johnson,

Ben "Benny" Miller, Thornton Turner and Wesley Hodge. All will be remembered for their service to their country.

In these stories of African Americans in Northeast Philadelphia, it has been shown that blacks have always been a part of Northeast Philadelphia history. Long ago these citizens developed stable and industrious communities, and they have contributed many productive and patriotic citizens to the northeast.

BIBLIOGRAPHY

Burton, Katharine. *The Golden Door: The Life of Katharine Drexel.* New York: P.J. Kenedy & Sons, 1957.

DeFinis, Rudy. *The Holmesburg Book of Then & Now.* Philadelphia, PA: self-published, 2008.

Farley, James J. *Making Arms in the Machine Age: Philadelphia's Frankford Arsenal.* University Park: Pennsylvania State University Press, 1994.

Freitag, Alicia M., and Harry C. Silcox. *Historic Northeast Philadelphia.* Holland, PA: Brighton Press, 1994.

Friedman, Murray. *Philadelphia Jewish Life, 1940–2000.* Philadelphia, PA: Temple University Press, 2003.

Grapp, Johnna Frueh. *Fox Chase 300 Years of Memories.* Fox Chase, PA: Friends of Burholme and the Ryerss Museum, 1976.

Hotchkin, S.F., Reverend. *The Bristol Pike.* Philadelphia, PA: George W. Jacobs, 1893.

Iatarola, Louis M., and Lynn-Carmela T. Iatarola. *Lower Northeast Philadelphia.* Charleston, SC: Arcadia Publishing, 2008.

Iatarola, Louis M., and Siobhan Gephart. *Tacony.* Charleston, SC: Arcadia Publishing, 2000.

Karchin, Louis. *Old Northeast Philadelphia County 1609–1854.* Philadelphia, PA: Northeast High School Press, 1969.

Martindale, Joseph. *History of the Townships of Byberry and Moreland.* Philadelphia, PA: T. Ellwood Zell, 1867.

Rivinus, Marion Willis, and [Katharine] Hansell Biddle. *Lights Along the Delaware.* Philadelphia, PA: Dorrance Company, 1965.

Silcox, Harry C. *The History of Tacony Holmesburg, and Mayfair: An Intergenerational Study.* Holland, PA: Brighton Press, 1992.

———. *A Place to Live and Work: The Henry Disston Saw Works and the Tacony Community of Philadelphia.* University Park: Pennsylvania State University Press, 1994.

———. *Remembering Northeast Philadelphia.* Charleston, SC: The History Press, 2008.

Silcox, Harry C., and Lillian Lake. *Take a Trip Through Time: Northeast Philadelphia Revisited.* Holland, PA: Brighton Press, 1996.

Stopper, Pat Worthington. *A Pictorial Glimpse into the Past.* Holland, PA: Brighton Press, 1997. Pictures are of the Bustleton, Somerton and Byberry area.

———. *A Pictorial Glimpse into the Past II.* Holland, PA: self-published, 1997. More pictures of Bustleton, Somerton and Byberry.

Willits, Samuel C. *A History of Lower Dublin Academy.* Manuscript originally written in 1885. Philadelphia, PA: Trustees of the Lower Dublin Academy, 2009.

ABOUT THE AUTHORS

D r. Harry C. Silcox, longtime resident and historian of Northeast Philadelphia, was principal of Lincoln High School from 1976 to 1992. A basketball player at Lincoln High School in 1951, Silcox went on to become a Temple University star player in the mid-1950s. He received a doctorate in history from Temple University in 1972, having studied under Philadelphia historians Dennis Clark and Russell Weigley. He began studying the history of Northeast Philadelphia in 1978, writing the definitive history of Tacony in 1992, *A Place to Live and Work*, published by Penn State Press. Today, he writes the popular biweekly column in the *Northeast Times* entitled "Living in the Past."

F rank W. Hollingsworth's family has been in Northeast Philadelphia since the 1830s. He grew up in Torresdale in the 1950s and began studying the homes and archives connected to the life of the community. Over the years, Frank and his mother have

increased their collection of artifacts and information about Torresdale. He is recognized by all as a history buff who has greatly aided historians searching for information about the northeast. Currently, he is the community sponsor of the lecture series on Torresdale that focuses on the historic background and lifestyles of that community. Frank is a member of the Irish Center's Commodore Barry Memorial Library Committee and is active in the Philadelphia Irish community.

Visit us at
www.historypress.net

www.ingramcontent.com/pod-product-compliance
Lightning Source LLC
Chambersburg PA
CBHW060803100426

42813CB00004B/933